On the *Revival of the Religious Sciences* (*Iḥyāʾ ʿulūm al-dīn*)

"The *Iḥyāʾ ʿulūm al-dīn* is the most valuable and most beautiful of books."

—Ibn Khallikān (d. 681/1282)

"The *Iḥyāʾ ʿulūm al-dīn* is one of al-Ghazālī's best works."

—Aḥmad b. ʿAbd al-Ḥalīm (d. 728/1328)

"Any seeker of [felicity of] the hereafter cannot do without the *Iḥyāʾ ʿulūm al-dīn*"

—Tāj al-Dīn al-Subkī (d. 771/1370)

"The *Iḥyāʾ ʿulūm al-dīn* is a marvelous book containing a wide variety of Islamic sciences intermixed with many subtle accounts of Sufism and matters of the heart."

—Ibn Kathīr (d.774/1373)

"The *Iḥyāʾ ʿulūm al-dīn* is one of best and greatest books on admonition, it was said concerning it, 'if all the books of Islam were lost except for the *Iḥyāʾ* it would suffice what was lost.'"

—Ḥājjī Khalīfa Kātib Čelebī (d. 1067/1657)

"The *Iḥyāʾ* [*ʿulūm al-dīn*] is one of [Imām al-Ghazālī's] most noble works, his most famous work, and by far his greatest work'"

—Muḥammad Murtaḍā l-Zabīdī (d. 1205/1791)

On Imām al-Ghazālī

"Al-Ghazālī is [like] a deep ocean [of knowledge]."

—Imām al-Ḥaramayn al-Juwaynī (d. 478/1085)

"Al-Ghazālī is the second [Imām] Shāfiʿī."

—Muḥammad b. Yaḥyā l-Janzī (d. 549/1154)

"Abū Ḥāmid al-Ghazālī, the Proof of Islam (Ḥujjat al-Islām) and the Muslims, the Imām of the imāms of religion, [is a man] whose like eyes have not seen in eloquence and elucidation, and speech and thought, and acumen and natural ability."

—ʿAbd al-Ghāfir b. Ismāʿīl al-Fārisī (d. 529/1134)

"[He was] the Proof of Islam and Muslims, Imām of the imāms of religious sciences, one of vast knowledge, the wonder of the ages, the author of many works, and [a man] of extreme intelligence and the best of the sincere."

—Imām al-Dhahabī (d. 748/1347)

"Al-Ghazālī is without doubt the most remarkable figure in all Islam."

—T.J. DeBoer

". . . A man who stands on a level with Augustine and Luther in religious insight and intellectual vigor."

—H.A.R. Gibb

"I have to some extent found, and I believe others can find, in the words and example of al-Ghazālī a true *iḥyāʾ* . . ."

—Richard J. McCarthy, S.J.

The Forty Books of the Revival of the Religious Sciences (*Iḥyāʾ ʿulūm al-dīn*)

The Quarter of Worship

1 The Book of Knowledge
2 The Principles of the Creed
3 The Mysteries of Purification
4 The Mysteries of the Prayer
5 The Mysteries of Charity
6 The Mysteries of Fasting
7 The Mysteries of the Pilgrimage
8 The Etiquette of the Recitation of the Qurʾān
9 Invocations and Supplications
10 The Arrangement of the Litanies and the Exposition of the Night Vigil

The Quarter of Customs

11 The Proprieties of Eating
12 The Proprieties of Marriage
13 The Proprieties of Acquisition and Earning a Living
14 The Lawful and the Unlawful
15 The Proprieties of Friendship and Brotherhood
16 The Proprieties of Retreat
17 The Proprieties of Travel
18 The Proprieties of the Audition and Ecstasy
19 The Commanding of Right and the Forbidding of Wrong
20 The Proprieties of Living and the Prophetic Mannerisms

The Quarter of Perils

21 The Exposition of the Wonders of the Heart
22 Training the Soul, Refining the Character, and Treating the Ailments of the Heart
23 Overcoming the Two Desires
24 The Bane of the Tongue
25 The Censure of Anger, Malice, and Envy
26 The Censure of This World
27 The Censure of Greed and the Love of Wealth
28 The Censure of Fame and Hypocritical Ostentation
29 The Censure of Pride and Vanity
30 The Censure of Deceit

The Quarter of Deliverance

31 On Repentance
32 On Patience and Thankfulness
33 On Fear and Hope
34 On Poverty and Abstinence
35 On Unity and Trust
36 On Love, Longing, Intimacy, and Contentment
37 On Intention, Sincerity, and Truthfulness
38 On Vigilance and Accounting
39 On Contemplation
40 On the Remembrance of Death and the Hereafter

THE PRINCIPLES OF THE CREED

Kitāb Qawāʿid al-ʿaqāʾid

Book 2 of

The Revival of the Religious Sciences

Iḥyāʾ ʿulūm al-dīn

بِسۡمِ ٱللَّهِ ٱلرَّحۡمَٰنِ ٱلرَّحِيمِ

AL-GHAZĀLĪ

Kitāb QAWĀʿID AL-ʿAQĀʾID

THE PRINCIPLES OF THE CREED

BOOK 2 of the *Iḥyāʾ ʿulūm al-dīn*

THE REVIVAL OF THE RELIGIOUS SCIENCES

TRANSLATED *from the* ARABIC
by KHALID WILLIAMS
with an INTRODUCTION *and*
NOTES *by* JAMES PAVLIN

FONS VITAE
2016

The Principles of the Creed, Book 2 of
The Revival of the Religious Sciences first published in 2016 by

Fons Vitae
49 Mockingbird Valley Drive
Louisville, KY 40207 USA

www.fonsvitae.com

The Fons Vitae Ghazali Series
Library of Congress Control Number: 2015957357
ISBN 978-1-94-1610-16-9

Copyediting and indexing: Valerie Joy Turner
Book design and typesetting: www.scholarlytype.com
Text typeface: Adobe Minion Pro 11/13.5

Cover art courtesy of National Library of Egypt, Cairo.
Qurʾānic frontispiece to part 19. Written and illuminated by ʿAbdallāh b.
Muḥammad al-Ḥamadānī for Sultan Uljaytu 713/1313. Hamadan.

Printed in Canada

Contents

Editor's Note

THIS is the complete translation of the *Kitāb Qawāʿid al-ʿaqāʾid*, the *Principles of the Creed*, book 2 of the *Iḥyāʾ ʿulūm al-dīn* of Ḥujjat al-Islām, Abū Ḥāmid al-Ghazālī. It was translated from the newly published Arabic text by Dār al-Minhāj of Jedda (2011), which utilized additional manuscripts and early printed editions.

Arabic terms that appear in italics follow the transliteration system of the *International Journal of Middle East Studies*. Common era (CE) dates have been added. The blessings on prophets and others, as used by Imām al-Ghazālī, are represented in the original Arabic, as listed below.

Arabic	English	Usage
عَزَّوَجَلَّ	Mighty and majestic is He	On mention of God
سُبْحَانَهُ وَتَعَالَىٰ	Exalted and most high is He	Used together or separately
صَلَّىٱللَّهُ عَلَيْهِ وَسَلَّمَ	Blessings and peace of God be upon him	On mention of the Prophet Muḥammad
عَلَيْهِ ٱلسَّلَامُ	Peace be upon him	On mention of one
عَلَيْهِمُ ٱلسَّلَامُ	Peace be upon them	or more prophets
رَضِيَ ٱللَّهُ عَنْهُ	God be pleased with him	On mention of one or more
رَضِيَ ٱللَّهُ عَنْهُمْ	God be pleased with them	Companions of the Prophet
رَضِيَ ٱللَّهُ عَنْهَا	God be pleased with her	On mention of a female Companion of the Prophet
رَحِمَهُ ٱللَّهُ	God have mercy on him	On mention of someone who is deceased

This translation was reviewed against the Arabic by James Pavlin, who also translated the Arabic footnotes and references provided by the editors at Dār al-Minhāj. These footnotes include comments from Murtaḍā l-Zabīdī's *Ithḥāf* (a detailed commentary on the *Iḥyāʾ ʿulūm al-dīn*) and identify many of Imām al-Ghazālī's sources.

We have provided explanatory footnotes where necessary, and clarification in hard brackets in the text as needed. In addition, we have compiled a short biography of Imām al-Ghazālī with a chronology of important events in his life. This is followed by an extract from Imām al-Ghazālī's introduction to the *Iḥyāʾ ʿulūm al-dīn* by way of introduction to the *Revival of the Religious Sciences* for those reading Imām al-Ghazālī for the first time.

The topic of the creed is central to the Islamic belief system and therefore is a critical and sensitive matter. In matters of faith (*uṣūl al-dīn, ʿaqīda*) Sunnī Muslims fall into two schools of thought—the Ashʿarī/Māturīdī school and the *ahl al-ḥadīth*, or literalist school (more commonly known as the Salafī school). Imām al-Ghazālī navigated between these two schools, as did many key Muslim scholars, including Abū Ḥasan al-Ashʿarī before him and Ibn al-Jawzī, al-Nawawī, and Ibn Ḥajar al-ʿAsqalānī after him. Readers interested in additional information may consult such works as the *Creed of Imām al-Ṭaḥāwī* (translated by Hamza Yusuf, Zaytuna Institute, 2007) or Imām Abū Ḥanīfa's *al-Fiqh al-Akbar Explained* (translated by Abdur-Rahman ibn Yusuf, White Thread Press, 2004).

Yet we must also remember that Islam is not just a theology, it is a comprehensive way of life that involves both inward belief and outward action. The *ḥadīth* of Gabriel emphasizes that faith (*īmān*) is one third of the *dīn*; we must not lose sight of the remaining two thirds, namely submission (*islām*) and excellence (*iḥsān*).

Biography of Imām al-Ghazālī

He is Abū Ḥāmid Muḥammad b. Muḥammad b. Muḥammad b. Aḥmad al-Ghazālī al-Ṭūsī; he was born in 450/1058 in the village of Ṭābarān near Ṭūs (in northeast Iran) and he died there, at the age of fifty-five, in 505/1111. Muḥammad's father died when he and his younger brother Aḥmad were still young; their father left a little money for their education in the care of a Sufi friend of limited means. When the money ran out, their caretaker suggested that they enroll in a *madrasa*. The *madrasa* system meant they had a stipend, room, and board. Al-Ghazālī studied *fiqh* in his hometown under a Sufi named Aḥmad al-Rādhakānī; he then traveled to Jurjān and studied under Ismāʿīl b. Masʿada al-Ismāʿīlī (d. 477/1084).

On his journey home his caravan was overtaken by highway robbers who took all of their possessions. Al-Ghazālī went to the leader of the bandits and demanded his notebooks. The leader asked, what are these notebooks? Al-Ghazālī answered: "This is the knowledge that I traveled far to acquire," the leader acquiesced to al-Ghazālī's demands after stating: "If you claim that it is knowledge that you have, how can we take it away from you?" This incident left a lasting impression on the young scholar. Thereafter, he returned to Ṭūs for three years, where he committed to memory all that he had learned thus far.

In 469/1077 he traveled to Nīshāpūr to study with the leading scholar of his time, Imām al-Ḥaramayn al-Juwaynī (d. 478/1085), at the Niẓāmiyya College; al-Ghazālī remained his student for approximately eight years, until al-Juwaynī died. Al-Ghazālī was one of his most illustrious students, and al-Juwaynī referred to him as "a deep ocean [of knowledge]." As one of al-Juwaynī star pupils, al-Ghazālī used to fill in as a substitute lecturer in his teacher's absence. He also tutored his fellow students in the subjects that al-Juwaynī taught at the Niẓāmiyya. Al-Ghazālī wrote his first book, on the founding principles of legal theory (*uṣūl al-fiqh*), while studying with al-Juwaynī.

Very little is known about al-Ghazālī's family, though some biographers mention that he married while in Nīshāpūr; others note that he had married in Ṭūs prior to leaving for Nīshāpūr. Some accounts state that he had five children, a son who died early and four daughters. Accounts also indicate that his mother lived to see her son rise to fame and fortune.

After the death of al-Juwaynī, al-Ghazālī went to the camp (*al-muᶜaskar*) of the Saljūq *wazīr* Niẓām al-Mulk (d. 485/1192). He stayed at the camp, which was a gathering place for scholars, and quickly distinguished himself among their illustrious company. Niẓām al-Mulk recognized al-Ghazālī's genius and appointed him professor at the famed Niẓāmiyya College of Baghdad.

Al-Ghazālī left for Baghdad in 484/1091 and stayed there four years—it was a very exciting time to be in the heart of the Islamic empire. At the Niẓāmiyya College he had many students, by some estimates as many as three hundred. In terms of his scholarly output, this was also a prolific period in which he wrote *Maqāṣid al-falāsifa, Tahāfut al-falāsifa, al-Mustaẓhirī,* and other works.

Al-Ghazālī was well-connected politically and socially; we have evidence that he settled disputes related to the legitimacy of the rule of the ᶜAbbāsid caliph, al-Mustaẓhir (r. 487–512/1094–1118) who assumed his role as the caliph when he was just fifteen years old, after the death of his father al-Muqtadī (d. 487/1094). Al-Ghazālī issued a *fatwā* of approval of the appointment of al-Mustaẓhir and was present at the oath-taking ceremony.

In Baghdad, al-Ghazālī underwent a spiritual crisis, during which he was overcome by fear of the punishment of the hellfire. He became convinced that he was destined for the hellfire if he did not change his ways; he feared that he had become too engrossed in worldly affairs, to the detriment of his spiritual being. He began to question his true intentions: was he writing and teaching to serve God, or because he enjoyed the fame and fortune that resulted from his lectures. He experienced much suffering, both inward and outward; one day as he stood before his students to present a lecture, he found himself unable to speak. The physicians were unable to diagnose any physical malady. Al-Ghazālī remained in Baghdad for a time, then left his teaching post for the pilgrimage. He left behind fortune, fame, and influence. He was beloved by his numerous students and had many admirers, including the sultan; he was also envied by many. The presumption is that he left in the manner he did—ostensibly to undertake the pilgrimage—because if he had made public his intentions to leave permanently, those around him would have tried to convince him to remain and the temptation might have been too strong to resist.

After leaving Baghdad, he changed direction and headed toward Damascus; according to his autobiography he disappeared from the intellectual scene for ten years. This does not mean that he did not teach, but that he did not want to return to public life and be paid for teaching. This ten-year period can be divided into two phases. First, he spent two years in the East—in greater Syria and on the pilgrimage. We have evidence that while on his return to Ṭūs he appeared at a Sufi lodge opposite the Niẓāmiyya College in Baghdad. He spent the second phase of the ten-year period (the remaining eight years) in Ṭūs, where he wrote the famed *Iḥyāʾ ʿulūm al-dīn*, a work that was inspired by the change in his outlook that resulted from his spiritual crisis.

When he arrived back in his hometown in 490/1097, he established a school and a Sufi lodge, in order to continue teaching and learning. In 499/1106, Niẓām al-Mulk's son, Fakhr al-Mulk, requested that al-Ghazālī accept a teaching position at his old school, the Niẓāmiyya of Nīshāpūr. He accepted and taught for a time, but left this position in 500/1106 after Fakhr al-Mulk was assassinated by Ismāʿīlīs. He then returned to Ṭūs and divided his time between teaching and worship. He died in 505/1111 and was buried in a cemetery near the citadel of Ṭābarān.

Eulogies in Verse

Because of him the lame walked briskly,
And the songless through him burst into melody.

On the death of Imām al-Ghazālī, Abū l-Muẓaffar Muḥammad al-Abiwardī said of his loss:

> He is gone! and the greatest loss which ever afflicted me,
> was that of a man who left no one like him among mankind.

Legacy and Contributions of al-Ghazālī

Al-Ghazālī's two hundred and seventy-three works span many disciplines and can be grouped under the following headings:

1. Jurisprudence and legal theory. Al-Ghazālī made foundational contributions to Shāfiʿī jurisprudence; his book *al-Wajīz* is major handbook that has been used in teaching institutions around the world; many commentaries have been written on it, most notably by Abū l-Qāsim ʿAbd al-Karīm al-Rāfiʿī (d. 623/1226). In legal theory, *al-Mustaṣfa min ʿilm al-uṣūl* is considered one of five foundational texts in the discipline.
2. Logic and philosophy. Al-Ghazālī introduced logic in Islamic terms that jurists could understand and utilize. His works on philosophy include the *Tahāfut al-falāsifa*, which has been studied far beyond the Muslim world and has been the subject of numerous commentaries, discussions, and refutations.
3. Theology, including works on heresiography in refutation of Bāṭinī doctrines. He also expounded on the theory of occasionalism.
4. Ethics and educational theory. The *Mīzān al-ʿamal* and other works such as the *Iḥyāʾ ʿulūm al-dīn* mention a great deal on education.
5. Spirituality and Sufism. His magnum opus, the *Iḥyāʾ ʿulūm al-dīn* is a pioneering work in the field of spirituality, in terms of its organization and its comprehensive scope.
6. Various fields. Al-Ghazālī also wrote shorter works in a variety of disciplines, including his autobiography (*al-Munqidh min al-ḍalāl*), works on Qurʾānic studies (*Jawāhir al-Qurʾān*), and political statecraft (*Naṣiḥat al-mūluk*).

Chronology of al-Ghazālī's Life

450/1058	Birth of al-Ghazālī at Ṭūs
c. 461/1069	Began studies at Ṭūs
c. 465/1073	Traveled to Jurjān to study
466–469/1074–1077	Studied at Ṭūs
469/1077	Went to Nīshāpūr to study with al-Jūwaynī
473/1080	al-Ghazālī composed his first book, *al-Mankhūl.*
477/1084	Death of al-Fāramdhī, one of al-Ghazālī's teachers.
478/1085	Death of al-Jūwaynī; al-Ghazālī left Nīshāpūr
1 Jumāda 484/ July 1091	Arrival in Baghdad
4 Ramaḍān 485/ 14 October 1092	Assassination of Niẓām-al-Mulk
484–487/1091–1094	Study of philosophy begins
Rabīʿ II 486/June 1093	Present at lectures in the Niẓāmiyya
Muḥarrām 487/ February 1094	Present at the oath-taking of the new caliph, al-Mustaẓhir
487/1094	Finished *Maqāṣid al-falāsifa*
5 Muḥarrām 488/ 21 January 1095	Finished *Tahāfut al-falāsifa*
Rajab 488/ July 1095	Spiritual crisis
Dhū l-Qaʿda 488/ November 1095	Left Baghdad for Damascus
Dhū l-Qaʿda 489/ November – December 1096	Made pilgrimage and worked on the *Iḥyāʾ ʿulūm al-dīn*
Jumāda II 490/ May 1097	During a brief stop in Baghdad he taught from the *Iḥyāʾ ʿulūm al-dīn*
Rajab 490/June 1097	Abū Bakr b. al-ʿArabī saw him in Baghdad
Fall 490/1097	Leaves Baghdad for Khurasān

Dhū l-Ḥijja 490/ November 1097	Arrives in Khurasān, establishes *madrasa* in Ṭūs
Dhū l-Qaʿda 499/ July 1106	Returned to teaching in Nīshāpūr
500/1106	Wrote *al-Munqidh min al-ḍalāl*
500/1106	Returned to Ṭūs
28 Dhū l-Ḥijja 502/ 5 August 1109	Finished *al-Mustaṣfā*
Jumada I 505/ December 1111	Finished *Iljām*
7 Jumada II 505/ 18 December 1111	Death of al-Ghazālī at Ṭūs

About the *Revival of the Religious Sciences*

THE present work is book 2 of Imām al-Ghazālī's forty-volume masterpiece. Below is an excerpt from al-Ghazālī's introduction that explains the arrangement and purpose of the *Iḥyāʾ ʿulūm al-dīn*.

People have composed books concerning some of these ideas, but this book [the *Iḥyāʾ*] differs from them in five ways, by:

1. clarifying what they have obscured and elucidating what they have treated casually;
2. arranging what they scattered and putting in order what they separated;
3. abbreviating what they made lengthy and proving what they reported;
4. omitting what they have repeated; and
5. establishing the truth of certain obscure matters that are difficult to understand and which have not been presented in books at all.

For although all the scholars follow one course, there is no reason one should not proceed independently and bring to light something unknown, paying special attention to something his colleagues have forgotten. Or they are not heedless about calling attention to it, but they neglect to mention it in books. Or they do not overlook it, but something prevents them from exposing it [and making it clear].

So these are the special properties of this book, besides its inclusion of all these various kinds of knowledge.

Two things induced me to arrange this book in four parts. The first and fundamental motive is that this arrangement in establishing what is true and in making it understandable is, as it were, inevitable because the branch of knowledge by which one approaches the hereafter is divided into the knowledge of [proper] conduct and the knowledge of [spiritual] unveiling.

By the knowledge of [spiritual] unveiling I mean knowledge and only knowledge. By the science of [proper] conduct I mean knowledge as well as action in accordance with that knowledge. This work will deal only with the science of [proper] conduct, and not with [spiritual] unveiling, which one is not permitted to record in writing, although it is the ultimate aim of saints and the ultimate aim of the sincere. The science of [proper] conduct is merely a path that leads to unveiling and only through that path did the prophets of God communicate with the people and lead them to Him. Concerning [spiritual] unveiling, the prophets عَلَيْهِمُ السَّلَامُ spoke only figuratively and briefly through signs and symbols, because they realized the inability of people's minds to comprehend. Therefore since the scholars are heirs of the prophets, they cannot but follow in their footsteps and emulate their way.

The knowledge of [proper] conduct is divided into (1) outward knowledge, by which I mean knowledge of the senses and (2) inward knowledge, by which I mean knowledge of the functions of the heart.

The physical members either perform acts of prescribed worship, or acts that are in accordance with custom, while the heart, because it is removed from the senses and belongs to the world of dominion, is subject to either praiseworthy or blameworthy [influences]. Therefore it is necessary to divide this branch of knowledge into two parts: outward and inward. The outward part, which is connected to the senses, is subdivided into acts of worship and acts that pertain to custom. The inward part, which is connected to the states of the heart and the characteristics of the soul, is subdivided into blameworthy states and praiseworthy states. So the total makes four divisions of the sciences of the practice of religion.

The second motive [for this division] is that I have noticed the sincere interest of students in jurisprudence, which has become popular among those who do not fear God ﷻ but who seek to boast and exploit its influence and prestige in arguments. It [jurisprudence] is also divided into four quarters, and he who follows the style of one who is beloved becomes beloved.

Introduction

We begin Imām al-Ghazālī's essential work on the Islamic creed with two important and foundational *ḥadīths*. Imām al-Bukhārī dedicated a whole section of *al-Ṣaḥīḥ* to the topic of the unity (*tawḥīd*) of God. It includes a tradition that is a summary of the creed. When the Prophet صَلَّى ٱللَّهُ عَلَيْهِ وَسَلَّمَ sent Muʿadh to Yemen, Ibn ʿAbbās narrated that the Prophet said to Muʿadh,

> You are going to a nation from the people of the Book, so first invite them to [belief in] the unity (*tawḥīd*) of God. If they learn that, tell them that God has enjoined on them five prayers to be offered in one day and one night. And if they pray, tell them that God has enjoined on them *zakāt* of their properties and it is to be taken from the rich among them and given to the poor. And if they agree to that, then take from them *zakāt* but avoid the best property of the people.

Imām Muslim also recognized that the creed is essential for all Muslims, so much so that he began *al-Ṣaḥīḥ* with a *ḥadīth* that sets the stage for the study of the creed and Islam—it conveys the heart of Islamic knowledge. We have included it here in its entirety, just as Imām Muslim cited it.

Imām Muslim related the following:

> On the authority of Yaḥyā b. Yaʿmur, the first [person] in Basra who discussed predestination (*qadr*) was Maʿbad al-Juhanī. Ḥumayd b. ʿAbd al-Raḥmān al-Ḥimyarī and I set out for pilgrimage (or *ʿumra*) and said: Should it happen that we come into contact with one of the Companions of the Messenger of God صَلَّى ٱللَّهُ عَلَيْهِ وَسَلَّمَ we shall ask him about the controversy regarding *qadr* (predestination). By chance we came across [Abū ʿAbd al-Raḥmān] ʿAbdallāh b. ʿUmar b. al-Khaṭṭāb while he was entering the mosque. My companion and I surrounded

him. One of us (stood) on his right and the other stood on his left. I expected my companion to authorize me to speak. I therefore said, Abū ʿAbd al-Raḥmān! There have appeared some people in our land who recite the Qurʾān and pursue knowledge. And then after talking about their affairs, [I] added: They [such people] claim that there is no such thing as predestination and events are not predestined.

He [ʿAbdallāh b. ʿUmar] said: When you happen to meet such people tell them that I have nothing to do with them and they have nothing to do with me. And verily they are in no way responsible for my [belief]. ʿAbdallāh b. ʿUmar swore by Him [the Lord and said]: If any one of them [i.e., who does not believe in predestination] had gold equal to the bulk of [the mountain] of Uḥud and spent it [in the way of God], God would not accept it unless he affirmed his faith in predestination.

He further said, My father, [commander of the faithful, Abū Ḥafṣ] ʿUmar b. al-Khaṭṭāb رَضِيَ ٱللَّهُ عَنْهُ said, "One day while we were sitting with the Messenger of God there appeared before us a man whose clothes were exceedingly white and whose hair was exceedingly black; no signs of traveling could be seen on him and none of us knew him. He walked up and sat down by the Prophet. Resting his knees against his and placing the palms of his hands on his thighs, he said: 'O Muḥammad, tell me about Islam.'"

The Messenger of God said: "Islam is to testify that there is no god but God and Muḥammad is the messenger of God, to perform the prayers, to pay the *zakāt*, to fast in Ramāḍan, and to make the pilgrimage to the House [Kaʿba] if you are able to do so."

He said: "You have spoken the truth," and we were amazed that he asked him and said that he had spoken the truth.

He said: "Then tell me about faith (*īmān*)."

He [Muḥammad] said, "It is to believe in God, His angels, His books, His messengers, and the Last Day, and to believe in predestination, both the good and the evil thereof."

He said, "You have spoken the truth." He said, "Then tell me about *iḥsān*."

He [Muḥammad] said, "It is to worship God as though you are seeing Him, and while you see Him not yet truly He sees you."

He said, "Then tell me about the Hour."

He [Muḥammad] said, "The one questioned about it knows no better than the questioner."

He said, "Then tell me about its signs."

He [Muḥammad] said, "That the slave girl will give birth to her mistress and that you will see the barefoot, naked, destitute herdsman competing in constructing lofty buildings."

Then he left and I stayed for a time. Then he said, "O ʿUmar, do you know who the questioner was?"

I [ʿUmar] said, "God and His messenger know best."
He said, "He was [the angel] Gabriel, who came to teach you your religion."

These issues of creed were the subject of lively debates in which almost every important aspect of faith was discussed. Sometimes these were theological debates that grew into political differences, while in other cases, political differences became theological issues. A case in point is the revolt against the fourth rightly-guided caliph ʿAlī b. Abī Ṭālib رَضِيَ ٱللَّهُ عَنْهُ, which is addressed below. Another case is the *miḥna*[1] that took placed during ʿAbbāsid rule. During this period (from 218/833 to 234/848), the beliefs of the scholars were tested on the issue of a single point of contention, the createdness of the Qurʾān. Although many scholars acceded, Imām Aḥmad b. Ḥanbal held fast to the view of the people of the *sunna* that the Qurʾān is uncreated; after being imprisoned and tortured for many years, he was finally released and honored.

In the *Principles of the Creed*, the second book of the Quarter of Worship of the *Revival of the Religious Sciences*, Abū Ḥāmid al-Ghazālī explains the fundamental beliefs of the people of the *sunna*. He presents these creedal statements in the context of the correct theological positions that a Muslim must have in order to

---

1 See the dated but still useful account in Patton, *Aḥmed Ibn Ḥanbal and the Miḥna*. Also see Ibn al-Jawzī, trans. Cooperson, *Virtues of the Imām Aḥmad ibn Ḥanbal*, 2:72–259.

maintain the proper faith in God, His revelation, His messengers, and all essential matters related to the hereafter. The scope of these beliefs includes the proper understanding of the nature of God, Muḥammad's status as a prophet, the virtues of his Companions, the events related to resurrection and judgment, and the nature of faith (*īmān*) itself. This presentation of beliefs goes beyond a mere list of creedal statements, for al-Ghazālī mentions the scriptural foundations in the Qurʾān and *ḥadīth* and refers to transmitted reports from the Companions and other early generations of Muslims who were among the community of the righteous predecessors. As part of his presentation, al-Ghazālī supports these beliefs with rational arguments from the established Ashʿarī theology of his time.[2] Although he warns about the limited effectiveness of theological discourse (*kalām*), he employs these arguments as part of his refutation of ideas that he considered deviations from the beliefs of the people of the *sunna*. In this second book of the *Iḥyāʾ ʿulūm al-dīn*, his arguments are primarily directed against the Muʿtazila.[3]

In this work, al-Ghazālī mentions some of the early theological groups directly and indicates the numerous incorrect beliefs they held. For example, he refers to the Khawārij and Qadariyya[4] in chapter 2, in the context of showing that some of the Companions engaged in limited debates with groups that disagreed with and fought against the main body of Muslims. The Khawārij were a group that broke away from the fourth rightly-guided caliph ʿAlī b. Abī Ṭālib رضي الله عنه and promoted the belief that grave sins nullify

---

2 For an overview of Muslim theological thought, see Pavlin, "Sunni Kalam and Theological Controversies," in Nasr andLeaman (eds.), *History of Islamic Philosophy*, 1:105–118.

3 For an overview of the Muʿtazila and their beliefs, see Sharif (ed.), *A History of Muslim Philosophy*, 1:199–220, and Gimaret, "Muʿtazila," *Encyclopaedia of Islam*, second ed., 7:783–793.

4 For a historical overview of the early theological groups, see Blankinship, "The Early Creed," in Winter, *The Cambridge Companion to Classical Islamic Theology*, 33–54. Note that early groups like the Khawārij and Muʿtazila were originally defined by their theological views, and later delved into political causes, whereas groups like the Rawāfiḍ, that include the Shīʿa and Fāṭimids (forerunners of the Ismāʿīlīs, Druze, and ʿAlawīs), had political causes that then evolved into theological sects.

faith. They then declared most Muslims to be apostates and carried out attacks against them. They were eventually defeated by ʿAlī b. Abī Ṭālib رضي الله عنه at the battle of Nahrawan.

The term Qadariyya refers to those who denied predestination and claimed that humans possess absolute free will. This group emerged in the first/seventh century out of the debates over predestination and free will. Al-Ghazālī defended the position of the people of the *sunna* that maintains God's creation of human acts and upholds the Ashʿarī belief in a person's acquisition of those acts.[5] Al-Ghazālī also mentions the Rawāfiḍ (various Shīʿī sects) because of their rejection of the first three rightly-guided caliphs. He refers to them in chapter 3, where he discusses the necessity of believing in the legitimacy of the four rightly-guided caliphs.

In chapter 4 al-Ghazālī mentions the Murjiʾa; they were a group that claimed that faith remains complete in the heart of a believer and is not affected by acts. Thus the Murjiʾa denied the position of the people of the *sunna* that al-Ghazālī advocated, the position that faith can increase and decrease. In this book, however, al-Ghazālī directs most of his attention to the Muʿtazila, whom he refers in chapters 2, 3, and 4. This was no doubt the case because of their continued presence and influence in his time.

While it is beyond the scope of this preface to fully explain the beliefs of the Muʿtazila, a summary of their main ideas is necessary given al-Ghazālī's frequent reference to those of their beliefs that were contrary to those of the people of the *sunna*. The Muʿtazila are known for five principles: their concept of "oneness" (*tawḥīd*), "justice" (*ʿadl*), "the position between the two positions" (*al-manzila bayna al-manzilatayn*), "promise and punishment" (*al-waʿid wa l-waʿīd*), and "commanding good and forbidding evil" (*al-amr bi-l-maʿrūf*

---

5 Acquisition of acts refers to the process whereby a person "acquires" an act that was created by God. Consider the example of a man picking up a book. A Muʿtazila view of this example would maintain that the man's act of picking up the book was his own, that God had no role in it. The Ashʿarīs believed that this (like everything) was an act created by God, and in order for a man to be held accountable for that act, he must acquire it by free will, in this example by intending to stretch out his hand to pick up the book, by the acquisition of the act (from God, which God allows), and by actually picking up the book.

wa-l-nahy ʿan al-munkar).[6] The Muʿtazilī concept of oneness is based on a denial of all God's attributes. They claimed that God's attributes such as knowledge, power, life, hearing, seeing, speech, will, and other attributes are not part of God's essence. Thus they also said that the Qurʾān is created and not above the creation. As for their principle of justice, it stemmed from their denial that God creates all things. In particular, the Muʿtazila did not believe that God creates the acts (whether good deeds or bad) of people. Ultimately, this doctrine led the Muʿtazila to advocate man's absolute free will to obey or disobey God, who then is obliged to reward or punish accordingly. This doctrine relates to the principle of the punishment of people in the hereafter, and is a denial of God's ability to forgive sinners and show mercy.[7] The Muʿtazila advocated the notion that God will not allow intercession on behalf of grave sinners and that He will not remove them from the hellfire.[8] The "position between the two positions" refers to the Muʿtazilī concept that grave sinners are neither believers nor disbelievers, but will nonetheless be in the hellfire. The practice of "commanding good and forbidding evil," something that the people of the *sunna* also believed in, refers to the practice of maintaining justice and opposing injustice by word and by action, according to one's ability. Al-Ghazālī responded to these Muʿtazilī beliefs by pointing out the ways in which they contradicted the creed of the people of the *sunna*.

---

6 These five principles of Muʿtazila thought are discussed by Watt, *Islamic Philosophy*, 46–55.

7 The matter becomes ever more complex if we expand on the example from note 5, as it might relate to God's justice and punishment. The Muʿtazila held that if the man stole the book, God would be bound to punish him for the act which was entirely his and He would not be able to forgive him (as this would be unjust), and if he came by the book lawfully, God would be bound to reward him. The Ashʿarīs, in this example, would hold that God is free to punish the man who stole the book, or forgive him (all for reasons that we may not grasp or know), and God is equally free to reward or punish the man who came by the book lawfully (again, for reasons we may not grasp or know).

8 According to Watt, *Islamic Philosophy*, 52, this is a minor principle of Muʿtazila thought; it follows the concepts of "oneness" and "justice." He refers to it as the doctrine of "the promise and the threat [punishment]" and mentions that the Muʿtazila remained close to the Khawārij on this point.

Al-Ghazālī divides the *Principles of the Creed* into four chapters. The first chapter, "An exposition of the creed of the people of the *sunna* [with regard to] the two testimonies of faith, which are one of the foundations of Islam" is a concise summary of the essential aspects of the Muslim creed.[9] In a sense it is an introduction to the broader topic. In describing the nature of God, al-Ghazālī mentions the divine attributes of unity, transcendence, life, omnipotence, knowledge, will, hearing, sight, speech, and acts. This is followed by the essential beliefs related to Muḥammad as a messenger, descriptions of the hereafter, including resurrection, paradise, hell, intercession, and the virtues of the Companions.

The second chapter is entitled "On imparting religious instruction gradually, and the stages and levels of conviction." This chapter covers a range of topics related to how to teach the creed mentioned in chapter 1. Al-Ghazālī first discusses a child's education. This is followed by a series of questions in which he presents arguments and counter-arguments on several core theological issues. The first question deals with the ruling on studying debate and theology. In this context, he gives statements of those who condemned theology, such as Mālik b. Anas, al-Shāfiʿī, Aḥmad b. Ḥanbal, Sufyān al-Thawrī, and the people of *ḥadīth* in general. He then presents arguments for and against it, an exposition of its harms and benefits, and the limitations of studying and teaching theology. The second question relates to the issue of outward and inward knowledge. Al-Ghazālī's response is a collection of statements from the Prophet, various Companions, and other famous luminaries, including many early Sufis, that relate to the inner dimensions of faith. This chapter concludes with a detailed explanation of the science of unveiling (*mukashāfa*).

After establishing that inner realities (*bāṭin*) cannot oppose the law or contradict outer realities (*ẓāhir*), he proceeds to describe five categories of the mysteries of knowledge. The first category is the subtle realities that only the elite can perceive, those that must not be divulged to others. The second category deals with mysteries,

9 Chapter 1 is also known as "Imām al-Ghazālī's creed." Scholars have written commentaries on this summary, among them that of Imām al-Zarrūq (d. 899/1493), published in Beirut in 2006.

such as predestination, that generally can be understood, though their details should not be divulged. The third category relates to mysteries that can be alluded to through symbolic language; these are mysteries that initiates may understand but others will not. The fourth category refers to the perception of things in general terms, and the practice of obtaining deeper realization through experience. The fifth category describes the conveying of insight through concrete terms and expressions that common people will take at face value while adepts will grasp the deeper meanings.

The third chapter is entitled "Shining proofs of the creed, entitled 'The Jerusalem epistle on the principles of the creed' (*al-Risāla al-qudsiyya*)." Al-Ghazālī divides this chapter into four pillars with ten foundations in each pillar; he presents a detailed examination[10] of the creed outlined in chapter 1. It will suffice here to mention the pillars and foundations.

The first pillar focuses on the recognition of God's essence, as outlined in ten foundations: (1) knowledge of God's existence, (2) that He is beginningless and eternal, and (3) He is endless; (4) knowledge that He is not a substance that occupies space, (5) that He is not a body composed of substance, or (6) He is not an accident; (7) knowledge that He transcends direction, (8) that is He not resident in any place, (9) that He can be seen, and (10) that He is One.

The second pillar concerns His attributes, as outlined in ten foundations: knowledge that (1) He is living (*ḥayyān*), (2) knowing (*ʿālimān*), (3) all-powerful (*qādirān*), (4) volitional (*muridān*), (5) hearing (*samīʿān*) and seeing (*baṣīrān*), and (6) speaking (*mutakalimān*); (7) that He is transcendently beyond being incarnate in any contingent thing; and (8) that His speech (*kalām*) [is beginningless], (9) His knowledge (*ʿilm*) [is beginningless], and (10) will (*irāda*) is beginningless (*qadīm*).

The third pillar concerns His acts, as outlined in ten foundations: (1) that human acts are created by God, and (2) are acquired by people, and (3) they are willed by God; (4) that He creates and originates freely through His grace; (5) that He is able to charge [people] with more than they can bear; (6) that He is able to cause the innocent

10 Chapter 3 has been singled out for commentary, one of the well-known commentaries is that of Ibn Abī l-Sharīf, *Kitāb al-Musāmara fī sharḥ al-musāyyira*.

to suffer; (7) that He is not obliged to do what is most beneficial; (8) that only the law can impose obligations; (9) that it is [rationally] possible for Him to send prophets; and (10) that the prophethood of Muḥammad is affirmed and supported by miracles.

The fourth pillar pertains to things known by transmitted reports, as outlined in ten foundations: (1) the affirmation of the resurrection and reckoning, (2) the punishment of the grave, (3) the questions of Munkar and Nakīr, (4) the balance, (5) the traverse (*ṣirāṭ*), (6) paradise (*janna*) and the fire, (7) the rulings pertaining to the *imām*, (8) the virtues of the Companions, (9) the conditions of [political rule] of the *imāma*, and (10) [the affirmation] that even if a potential *imām* does not possess piety and knowledge, his rule is valid if he fulfills the other conditions.

The fourth chapter is entitled "On faith (*īmān*) and Islam, what connects and separates them, whether faith can increase and decrease, and whether the predecessors qualified their claims to faith [by saying "God willing"]. The topics are presented in a series of questions. The first discussion relates to whether the concept of Islam is identical with that of faith (*īmān*). Al-Ghazālī approaches this topic through three considerations: linguistically, by examining the meaning of the terms, their application in the law, and then legal rulings in regard to them. The second discussion concerns the issue of whether faith can increase and decrease. Here he looks into the different uses of the word faith, as belief in the heart with the sense of conviction, as belief and action taken together, and as belief by disclosure, the expansion of the breast, and the witnessing of the light of insight. The third discussion regards whether it is acceptable to say, "I am a believer, God willing." Al-Ghazālī responds to this by saying that this qualification is valid and has four justifications: two that pertain to doubt, not in faith itself, but in its final end or its perfection; the other two do not pertain to doubt at all. With the clarification of these four justifications, al-Ghazālī completes the second book of the Quarter of Worship of the *Revival of the Religious Sciences.*

In the name of God, the Merciful, the Compassionate

The Principles of the Creed

It is composed of four chapters[1]

Chapter 1: An exposition of the creed[2] of the people of the *sunna* [with regard to] the two testimonies of faith, which are one of the foundations of Islam.

Chapter 2: On imparting religious instruction gradually, and the stages and levels of conviction.

Chapter 3: Shining proofs of the creed, entitled "The Jerusalem epistle on the principles of the creed" (*al-Risāla al-qudsiyya fī qawāʿid al-ʿaqāʾid*).

Chapter 4: On faith (*īmān*) and Islam, what connects and separates them, whether faith can increase and decrease, and whether the predecessors qualified their claims to faith [by saying "God willing"].

1 The text on this page was compiled from Imām al-Ghazālī's chapter titles. The original text does not have a list of contents.

2 This chapter is known as Imām al-Ghazālī's creed.

1

An Exposition of the Creed of the People of the *Sunna* [with regard to] the Two Testimonies of Faith, which are One of the Foundations of Islam

We say, and all success is with God: Praise be to God, the Beginner, the Restorer, He who does what He wills, Possessor of the glorious throne and intense force; He who guides His pure servants to the right way and the firm path; He who blesses them, after their attestation to His unity, by guarding their creed from the darkness of doubt and uncertainty; He who steers them toward the emulation of His Messenger, the chosen Prophet Muḥammad صَلَّى ٱللَّٰهُ عَلَيْهِ وَسَلَّمَ, and aids and strengthens them in following the tracks of his noble honored Companions; He who manifests Himself to them in His essence and acts through the beautiful qualities of His attributes, which can only be perceived by *he who listens while he is present* [*in mind*] [50:37].

الْفَصْلُ الْأَوَّلَ

فِي تَرْجَمَةِ عَقِيدَةِ أَهْلِ السُّنَّةِ
فِي كَلِمَتِي الشَّهَادَةِ الَّتِي هِيَ
أَحَدَ مَبَانِي الْإِسْلَامِ

فَنَقُولُ وَبِاللهِ التَّوْفِيقِ : الحمدُ للهِ المبدئِ المعيدِ ، الفعَّالِ لما يريدُ ، ذي العرشِ المجيدِ ، والبطشِ الشديدِ ، الهادي صفوةَ العبيدِ ، إلى المنهجِ الرشيدِ ، والمسلكِ السديدِ ، المنعمِ عليهِمْ بعدَ شهادةِ التوحيدِ بحراسةِ عقائدِهِمْ عنْ ظلماتِ التشكيكِ والترديدِ ، السالك بهم إلى اتِّباعِ رسولهِ المصطفى مُحَمَّدٍ صَلَّى اللَّهُ عَلَيْهِ وَسَلَّمَ ، واقتفاءِ آثار صحبِهِ الأكرمينَ المكرَّمينَ بالتأييدِ والتسديدِ ، المتجلِّي لهُمْ في ذاتِهِ وأفعالِهِ بمحاسنِ أوصافِهِ التي لا يدركُها إلا مَنْ ألقى السمعَ وهوَ شهيدٌ.

Unity

He discloses and informs them that He is One in His essence without partner, unique without likeness, absolute without opposite, singular without rival. He is eternal without a predecessor, timeless without beginning, ever-being without end, everlasting without termination, all-sustaining without interruption, constant without waning. He is, was, and ever will be endowed with the qualities of majesty, and the interval of time and passing of lifespans will never bring Him to an end. Rather, *He is the First and the Last, the Outward and the Inward. And He is, of all things, knowing* [57:3].

Transcendence

He is not a bodily form, nor a limited quantitative substance. He does not resemble bodies whether in a quantifiable or divisible [amount]. He is not a substance, nor a locus for substances. He is not an accident, nor a locus for accidents. Indeed, He does not resemble any being, nor does any being resemble Him. *There is nothing like unto Him* [42:11], nor is He like anything. He is not constrained by measure, confined by physical dimensions or surrounded by spatial directions. All the earths and all the heavens cannot hold Him.

He is ascendant over His throne in the way He says that He is, according to the sense He intends—ascendant in a manner transcending all notions of physical contact, settling, position, indwelling, or movement. The throne does not bear him; rather, the throne and its bearers are borne by His subtle power and are powerless in His grasp.

التَّوْحِيــــــدُ

المعرِّفِ إِيَّاهُمْ أَنَّهُ في ذاتِهِ واحدٌ لا شريكَ لهُ، فردٌ لا مثيلَ لهُ، صمدٌ لا ضدَّ لهُ، منفردٌ لا ندَّ لهُ، وأَنَّهُ قديمٌ لا أوَّلَ لهُ أزليٌّ لا بدايةَ لهُ مستمرُّ الوجودِ لا آخرَ لهُ أبديٌّ لا نهايةَ لهُ قيُّومٌ لا انقطاعَ لهُ دائمٌ لا انصرامَ لهُ، لمْ يزلْ ولا يزالُ موصوفاً بنعوتِ الجلالِ لا يَقضي عليهِ بالانقضاءِ تصرُّمُ الآمادِ وانقراضُ الآجالِ، بل ﴿هُوَ ٱلۡأَوَّلُ وَٱلۡأٓخِرُ وَٱلظَّٰهِرُ وَٱلۡبَاطِنُۖ وَهُوَ بِكُلِّ شَيۡءٍ عَلِيمٌ ٣﴾. [سُورَةُ الحَدِيدِ: ٣]

التَّنْزِيــــــه

وأنَّه ليسَ بجسمٍ مصوَّرٍ ولا جوهرٍ محدودٍ مقدَّرٍ، وأنَّهُ لا يماثلُ الأجسامَ، ولا في التقديرِ ولا في قَبولِ الانقسامِ، وأنَّهُ ليسَ بجوهرٍ ولا تَحِلُّهُ الجواهرُ، ولا بعَرَضٍ ولا تَحِلُّهُ الأعراضُ، بلْ لا يماثلُ موجوداً ولا يماثلُهُ موجودٌ، و ﴿لَيۡسَ كَمِثۡلِهِۦ شَيۡءٞۖ﴾ [سُورَةُ الشُّورَىٰ: ١١] ولا هوَ مثْلُ شيءٍ. وأنَّهُ لا يحدُّهُ المقدارُ، ولا تحويهِ الأقطارُ، ولا تحيطُ بهِ الجهاتُ، ولا تكتنفُهُ الأرضونَ ولا السمواتُ.

وأنَّهُ مستوٍ على العرشِ على الوجْهِ الذي قالَهُ وبالمعنى الذي أرادَهُ، استواءً منزَّهاً عنِ المماسَّةِ والاستقرارِ، والتمكُّنِ والحلولِ والانتقالِ، لا يحملُهُ العرْشُ، بلِ العرْشُ وحملتُهُ محمولونَ بلطْفِ قدرتِهِ، ومقهورونَ في قبضتِهِ.

He is above the throne and the heavens, and above everything as far as the stars reach—above them in a way that does not make Him any nearer to the throne or the heavens, nor any further from the earth and the stars. Rather, He is exalted in degree above the throne and the heavens just as He is exalted in degree above the earth and the stars. Yet despite this, He is near to all things, and nearer to His servants than their own carotid artery, and *He is witness to all things* [34:47].

His nearness no more resembles the nearness of physical objects than His essence resembles the essences of physical objects.

He is not incarnate in anything, and nothing is incarnate in Him. He is too exalted to be contained by space, too holy to be confined by time. Before He created time and space, He was; and He is now ever as He was.

He is distinguished from His creation by His attributes. There is nothing in His essence (*dhāt*) but Him, and His being is not in anything but Him.

He is too holy to be affected by change and motion. He is unaffected by events, unchanged by accidents. Rather, He never ceases to be in His qualities of majesty transcending cessation, and in His attributes of perfection, beyond needing any increase in perfection.

His existence can be discerned by the intelligence, and His essence can be seen with the eye as a blessed favor from Him, and a kindness to the righteous in the abode of perpetuity, to perfect their bliss with the sight of His holy countenance.

وهوَ فوقَ العرْشِ والسماءِ ، وفوْقَ كلِّ شيءٍ إلىٰ تخومِ الثرىٰ ، فوقيةً لا تزيدُهُ قرباً إلى العرشِ والسماءِ ، كما لا تزيدُهُ بعداً عن الأرضِ والثرىٰ بلْ هوَ رفيعُ الدرجاتِ عنِ العرشِ والسماءِ ، كما أنَّهُ رفيعُ الدرجاتِ عنِ الأرضِ والثرىٰ. وهوَ معَ ذلكَ قريبٌ مِنْ كلِّ موجودٍ ، وهوَ أقربُ إلى العبيدِ مِنْ حبْلِ الوريدِ ، ﴿وَهُوَ عَلَىٰ كُلِّ شَىْءٍ شَهِيدٌ﴾ [سُورَةُ سَبَإٍ: ٤٧]

إذْ لا يماثلُ قربُهُ قرْبَ الأجسامِ ، كما لا تماثلُ ذاتُهُ ذاتَ الأجسامِ .

وأنَّهُ لا يحلُّ في شيءٍ ، ولا يحلُّ فيهِ شيءٌ ، تعالىٰ عنْ أنْ يحويَهُ مكانٌ ، كما تقدَّسَ عنْ أنْ يحدَّهُ زمانٌ ، بلْ كانَ قبْلَ أنْ خلَقَ الزمانَ والمكانَ ، وهوَ الآنَ علىٰ ما عليهِ كانَ .

وأنَّهُ بائنٌ منْ خلقِهِ بصفاتِهِ ، ليسَ في ذاتِهِ سواهُ ، ولا في سواهُ ذاتُهُ .

وأنَّهُ مقدسٌ عنِ التغيُّرِ والانتقالِ ، لا تحُلُّهُ الحوادثُ ، ولا تعتريهِ العوارضُ ، بلْ لا يزالُ في نعوتِ جلالِهِ منزَّهاً عن الزوالِ ، وفي صفاتِ كمالِهِ مستغنياً عنْ زيادةِ الاستكمالِ .

وأنَّهُ في ذاتِهِ معلومُ الوجودِ بالعقولِ ، مرئِيُّ الذاتِ بالأبصارِ ، نعمةً منهُ ولطفاً بالأبرارِ في دارِ القرارِ ، وإتماماً منهُ للنعيمِ بالنظرِ إلىٰ وجهِهِ الكريمِ .

Life and Omnipotence

He تَعَالَىٰ is Alive, Omnipotent (*qādir*), Irresistible (*jabbār*), Overpowering (*qāhir*). Neither deficiency nor weakness can afflict Him. *Neither drowsiness overtakes Him nor sleep* [2:255]. Neither annihilation nor death can oppose Him.

To Him belong the worldly kingdom (*mulk*) and the spiritual domain (*malakūt*), and all glory and omnipotence. He possesses authority and control, creation and command. *And the heavens will be folded in His right hand* [39:67]. All creatures are powerless in his grasp.

He is the sole Creator and Maker, unique in possessing the power to bring [things] into being and originate [them]. He created all creatures and their actions, and decreed their provisions and their lifespans. Nothing can escape His grasp, and nothing happens against His will. His decrees are countless, His knowledge infinite.

Knowledge

He knows all that can be known, and encompasses all that occurs from the depths of the earth to the highest heavens. He is All-Knowing: not an atom's weight of information escapes His knowledge, whether on earth or in the heavens. He knows when a black ant creeps across a great rock on a dark night. He discerns the motion of a seed floating on the wind. *He knows the secret and what is* [*even*] *more hidden* [20:7]. He is aware of the subtle notions of the conscience, the wanderings of the mind, and the best-kept secrets. He knows all this with an eternal timeless knowledge that has never ceased being His attribute through all eternity, not with newly-acquired knowledge that resides in and alters His essence.

الْحَيَاةُ وَالْقُدْرَةُ

وأَنَّهُ تعالىٰ حيٌّ قادرٌ، جبَّارٌ قاهرٌ، لا يعتريهِ قصورٌ ولا عجْزٌ، ولا تأخذُهُ سِنَةٌ ولا نومٌ، ولا يعارضُهُ فناءٌ ولا موتٌ.

وأَنَّهُ ذو الملْكِ والملكوتِ، والعزَّةِ والجبروتِ، لهُ السلطانُ والقهرُ، والخلْقُ والأمرُ، وَٱلسَّمَٰوَٰتُ مَطْوِيَّٰتُۢ بِيَمِينِهِۦۚ، والخلائقُ مقهورونَ في قبضتِهِ.

وأَنَّهُ المتفرِّدُ بالخلْقِ والاختراعِ المتوحِّدُ بالإيجادِ والإبداعِ خلَقَ الخلْقَ وأعمالَهُمْ، وقدَّرَ أرزاقَهُمْ وآجالَهُمْ، لا يشُذُّ عنْ قبضتِهِ مقدورٌ، ولا يعزُبُ عنْ قدرتِهِ تصاريفُ الأمورِ، لا تُحصَىٰ مقدوراتُهُ ولا تتناهىٰ معلوماتُهُ.

الْعَـلْمُ

وأَنَّهُ عالمٌ بجميعِ المعلوماتِ، محيطٌ بما يجري مِنْ تخومِ الأرضينَ إلىٰ أعلى السمواتِ، وأنَّهُ عالمٌ لا يعزُبُ عنْ علمِهِ مثقالُ ذرَّةٍ في الأرضِ ولا في السماءِ، بلْ يعلمُ دبيبَ النملةِ السوداءِ، على الصخرةِ الصمَّاءِ، في الليلةِ الظلماءِ، ويُدركُ حركةَ الذرِّ في جوِّ الهواءِ، وَيَعْلَمُ ٱلسِّرَّ وَأَخْفَى، ويطَّلعُ علىٰ هواجِسِ الضمائرِ، وحركاتِ الخواطرِ، وخفيَّاتِ السرائرِ، بعلْمٍ قديمٍ أزليٍّ لمْ يزلْ موصوفاً بهِ في أزلِ الآزالِ، لا بعلْمٍ متجدِّدٍ حاصِلٍ في ذاتِهِ بالحلولِ والانتقالِ.

Will

He سُبۡحَانَهُ wills all things that exist and arranges all that happens. Nothing occurs in the worldly kingdom or the spiritual domain, being few or many, small or large, good or evil, beneficial or harmful, [of] faith or disbelief, acknowledgment or denial, victory or failure, increase or decrease, obedience or disobedience, except by His decree and predestination, and His wisdom and will. If He wills something, it comes to pass; if He does not will it, it does not. Not a single glance or passing thought is outside His will. He is the Initiator (*mubdi*ʾ), the Restorer, He who does what He wills. Nothing can rebuff His command, nor turn back His decree. No servant of His can avoid disobeying Him save by the success and grace He gives, nor have the power to obey Him save by His will and desire. If all human beings, jinn, angels, and devils made a joint effort to move a single atom of the universe or keep it still against His desire and will, they would not be able to do it.

His will exists in His essence like the rest of His attributes. As such He never ceases to be attributed with it, and He never ceases to will in His eternity the existence of things in the times He destined for them, and they have always come to exist in their times just as He intended it in His eternity, not a moment sooner or later. They have always occurred in accordance to His knowledge and will without any substitution or change. He arranged all things, but not by thinking or planning over time, which is why no one thing can distract Him from any other.

الإِرَادَةُ

وأَنَّهُ سبحانَهُ مريدٌ للكائناتِ ، مدبِّرٌ للحادثاتِ ، فلا يجري في المُلْكِ والملكوتِ قليلٌ أَوْ كثيرٌ ، صغيرٌ أَوْ كبيرٌ ، خيرٌ أَوْ شرٌ ، نفعٌ أو ضرٌّ ، إيمانٌ أَوْ كفرٌ ، عرفانٌ أَوْ نكرٌ ، فوزٌ أَوْ خسْرانٌ ، زيادةٌ أَوْ نقصانٌ ، طاعةٌ أَوْ عصيانٌ . . إلا بقضائِهِ وقدَرِهِ ، وحكمتِهِ ومشيئتِهِ ، فما شاءَ . . كانَ ، وما لمْ يشأْ . . لمْ يكنْ ، لا يخرجُ عنْ مشيئتِهِ لفتةُ ناظرٍ ، ولا فلتَةُ خاطرٍ ، بلْ هوَ المبدئُ المعيدُ ، الفعَّالُ لما يريدُ ، لا رادَّ لأمرِهِ ، ولا معقِّبَ لقضائِهِ ، ولا مهربَ لعبدٍ عنْ معصيتِهِ إلا بتوفيقِهِ ورحمتِهِ ، ولا قوَّةَ لهُ علىٰ طاعتِهِ إلا بمشيئتهِ وإرادتِهِ ، فلوِ اجتمعَ الإنْسُ والجنُّ والملائكةُ والشياطينُ علىٰ أنْ يحرِّكوا في العالمِ ذرَّةً أَوْ يسكِّنوها دونَ إرادتِهِ ومشيئتِهِ . . لعجزوا .

وأنَّ إرادتَهُ قائمةٌ بذاتِهِ في جملةِ صفاتِهِ ، لمْ يزلْ كذلكَ موصوفاً بها ، مريداً في أزلِهِ لوجودِ الأشياءِ في أوقاتِها التي قدَّرَها ، فوُجدتْ في أوقاتِها كما أرادَهُ في أزلِهِ مِنْ غيرِ تقدُّمٍ ولا تأخُّرٍ ، بلْ وقعتْ علىٰ وَفْقِ علمِهِ وإرادتِهِ مِنْ غيرِ تبدُّلٍ ولا تغيُّرٍ ، دبَّرَ الأمورَ لا بترتيبِ أفكارٍ و تربُّصِ زمانٍ ، فلذلكَ لمْ يشغلْهُ شانٌ عن شانٍ.

Hearing and Sight

He تَعَالَىٰ is all-hearing and all-seeing. He hears and sees, and nothing audible escapes His hearing no matter how quiet, nor does anything visible escape His vision no matter how small. Distance does not obscure His hearing, nor does darkness veil His sight. He sees without pupil or eyelids, and hears without ear canals or ears, just as He knows without a heart, grasps without limbs, and creates without tools. His attributes no more resemble those of His creatures than His essence resembles the essences of His creatures.

Speech

He commands, prohibits, promises, and warns with a timeless and eternal speech that exists in His essence. It does not resemble the speech of His creatures for it is not a voice made by the passage of air and the movement of body parts, nor is it composed of letters articulated by the lips or tongue.

The Qurʾān, Torah, Gospel, and Psalms are the books He revealed to His messengers عَلَيْهِمُ ٱلسَّلَامُ. The Qurʾān is recited with tongues, written in books, and memorized in hearts, yet despite this it is eternally established in the essence of God تَعَالَىٰ, and undergoes no division or separation when it is transferred to hearts or pages. Moses عَلَيْهِ ٱلسَّلَامُ heard the speech of God تَعَالَىٰ without any voice or letter, just as the righteous will see the essence of God تَعَالَىٰ without any substance or accident.

السَّمْــعُ وَالْبَــصَرُ

وأنَّهُ تَعَالَىٰ سميعٌ بصيرٌ، يسمعُ ويرىٰ، لا يعزُبُ عنْ سمعِهِ مسموعٌ وإنْ خَفِيَ، ولا يغيبُ عنْ رؤيتِهِ مرئيٌّ وإنْ دقَّ، ولا يحجبُ سمعَهُ بُعْدٌ، ولا يدفعُ رؤيتَهُ ظلامٌ، يرىٰ مِنْ غيرِ حدقةٍ وأجفانٍ، ويسمعُ مِنْ غيرِ أصمخةٍ وآذانٍ، كما يعلمُ بغيرِ قلبٍ، ويبطشُ بغيرِ جارحةٍ، ويخلُقُ بغيرِ آلةٍ؛ إذْ لا تشبهُ صفاتُهُ صفاتِ الخلْقِ، كما لا تشبهُ ذاتُهُ ذواتِ الخلْقِ.

الْكَــلَامُ

وأنَّهُ تَعَالَىٰ متكلِّمٌ آمرٌ ناهٍ، واعدٌ متوعِّدٌ، بكلامٍ أزليٍّ قديمٍ قائمٍ بذاتِهِ، لا يشبهُ كلامَ الخلْقِ؛ فليسَ بصوتٍ يحدثُ مِنِ انسلالِ هواءٍ أو اصطكاكِ أجرامٍ، ولا بحرفٍ ينقطعُ بإطباقِ شَفَةٍ أَوْ تحريكِ لسانٍ.

وأنَّ القرآنَ والتوراةَ والإنجيلَ والزبورَ كتبُهُ المنزَّلَةُ علىٰ رسلِهِ عليهِمُ السَّلَامُ، وأنَّ القرآنَ مقروءٌ بالألسنةِ، مكتوبٌ في المصاحفِ، محفوظٌ في القلوبِ، وأنَّهُ معَ ذلكَ قديمٌ قائمٌ بذاتِ اللهِ تَعَالَىٰ، لا يقبلُ الانفصالَ والافتراقَ، بالانتقالِ إلى القلوبِ والأوراقِ، وأنَّ موسىٰ عَلَيْهِ ٱلسَّلَامُ سمعَ كلامَ اللهِ تَعَالَىٰ، بغيرِ صوتٍ ولا حرفٍ، كما يرى الأبرارُ ذاتَ اللهِ تَعَالَىٰ مِنْ غيرِ جوهرٍ ولا عرضٍ.

Given that He possesses these attributes, this means He is Living, Knowing, Omnipotent, Volitional, Hearing, Seeing, and Speaking, with life, power, knowledge, will, hearing, sight, and speech, not merely by virtue of His essence.

Acts

Everything besides Him سُبْحَانَهُ وَتَعَالَىٰ exists through His acts and proceeds forth from His justice in the best, most perfect, most complete, and most equitable way. He is wise in His acts, equitable in His decrees. His justice is not analogous to the justice of human beings, for it is conceivable that a person is unjust by the inequitable disposal of what belongs to others, but it is inconceivable that God عَزَّوَجَلَّ could be unjust, since nothing belongs to anyone but Him such that He could dispose of it unjustly. Everything besides Him, be it jinn, human, devil, angel, sky, earth, animal, vegetable, mineral, substance, accident, intelligible, or tangible [thing], is a contingent being that He originated through His power after it had been non-existent; He produced it after it was nothing. Before time, only He existed, and there was nothing else; and then He made all creation as a manifestation of His power and a realization of what proceeds from His will and what is true in eternity of His word; He did not do it because He required or needed anything in creation.

He creates, originates, and teaches out of grace, not obligation; He extends favors and blessings freely, not out of duty. He did all this out of grace, generosity, kindness, and favor; He could easily have loosed all manner of torment upon His servants and tried them with every kind of pain and suffering—and had He done so, it would still have been equitable on His part, and not wicked or unjust.

وإذْ كانتْ لهُ هٰذهِ الصفاتُ . . كانَ حيّاً ، عالماً ، قادراً ، مريداً ، سميعاً ، بصيراً ، متكلِّماً ، بالحياةِ ، والقدرةِ ، والعلمِ ، والإرادةِ ، والسمعِ ، والبصرِ ، والكلامِ ، لا بمجرَّدِ الذاتِ .

الْأَفْعَالُ

وأنَّهُ سُبْحَانَهُ وَتَعَالَىٰ لا موجودَ سواهُ إلا وهوَ حادثٌ بفعلِهِ ، وفائضٌ مِنْ عدلِهِ ، علىٰ أحسنِ الوجوهِ وأكملِها ، وأتمِّها وأعدلِها ، وأنَّهُ حكيمٌ في أفعالِهِ ، عادلٌ في أقضيتِهِ ، لا يُقاسُ عدلُهُ بعدْلِ العبادِ ؛ إذِ العبدُ يُتصوَّرُ منهُ الظلْمُ بتصرُّفِهِ في ملْكِ غيرِهِ ، ولا يُتصوَّرُ الظلْمُ مِنَ اللهِ عَزَّ وَجَلَّ ؛ فإنّهُ لا يصادفُ لغيرِهِ ملكاً حتَّىٰ يكونَ تصرُّفُهُ فيهِ ظلْماً ، فكلُّ ما سواهُ مِنْ جنٍّ وإنسٍ ، وشيطانٍ ومَلَكٍ ، وسماءٍ وأرضٍ ، وحيوانٍ ونباتٍ وجمادٍ ، وجوهرٍ وعرضٍ ، ومدرَكٍ ومحسوسٍ . . حادثٌ اخترعَهُ بقدرتِهِ بعدَ العدمِ اختراعاً ، وأنشأَهُ إنشاءً بعدَ أنْ لمْ يكنْ شيئاً ؛ إذْ كانَ في الأزلِ موجوداً وحدَهُ ولمْ يكنْ معَهُ غيرُهُ ، فأحدثَ الخلْقَ بعدَ ذلكَ إظهاراً لقدرتِهِ ، وتحقيقاً لما سبقَ مِنْ إرادتِهِ ، ولما حَقَّ في الأزلِ مِنْ كلمتِهِ ، لا لافتقارِهِ إليهِ وحاجتِهِ .

وأنَّهُ متفضِّلٌ بالخلْقِ والاختراعِ والتكليفِ لا عنْ وجوبٍ ، ومتطوِّلٌ بالإنعامِ والإصلاحِ لا عنْ لزومٍ ، فلهُ الفضْلُ والإحسانُ ، والنعمةُ والامتنانُ ، إذْ كانَ قادراً علىٰ أنْ يصبَّ علىٰ عبادِهِ أنواعَ العذابِ ، ويبتليَهُمْ بضروبِ الآلامِ والأوصابِ ، ولوْ فعلَ ذلكَ . . لكانَ منهُ عدلاً ، ولمْ يكنْ قبيحاً ولا ظلماً .

He عَزَّوَجَلَّ rewards His faithful servants for obedience because of [His] generosity and promise, not because of [their] worthiness and [His] obligation. He is not obliged to do anything for anyone, nor is it conceivable that He could be unjust. He does not owe anything to anyone.

The obligation of His creatures to obey Him has been established by the words of His prophets عَلَيْهِمُ السَّلَامُ, not by human reason alone. Rather, He sent the messengers and proved their truthfulness with clear miracles, and they conveyed His commandments, prohibitions, promises, and warnings. It is obligatory for mankind to believe in what they have conveyed.

The Meaning of the Second Testimony [of Faith] is Bearing Witness to the Messenger of the Message

He sent the unlettered Qurayshī prophet, Muḥammad صَلَّى ٱللَّهُ عَلَيْهِ وَسَلَّمَ, with His message to all Arabs and non-Arabs, to all jinn and human beings. His law abrogated the previous laws, apart from those parts of them that it affirmed. He preferred him over the other prophets and made him the leader of humankind, and decreed that belief in the testimony of [God's] unity, "There is no god but God," is incomplete unless accompanied by the testimony [of belief in] the Messenger, "Muḥammad is the Messenger of God."

He holds mankind responsible for believing in him and in all the tidings he conveyed about this world and the hereafter, and does not accept the faith of any person until that person also has faith in what the Prophet conveyed about the events of the hereafter, beginning with the questions of Munkar and Nakīr, two terrible and awe-inspiring figures who will sit with each person

وأنَّهُ عَزَّ وَجَلَّ يثيبُ عبادَهُ المؤمنينَ على الطاعاتِ بحكمِ الكرمِ والوعْدِ ، لا بحكمِ الاستحقاقِ واللزومِ ؛ إذْ لا يجبُ عليهِ لأحدٍ فعْلٌ ، ولا يُتصوَّرُ منهُ ظلْمٌ ، ولا يجبُ لأحدٍ عليهِ حقٌّ .

وأنَّ حقَّهُ في الطاعاتِ وجبَ على الخلْقِ بإيجابِهِ على ألسنةِ أنبيائِهِ عَلَيْهِمُ السَّلَامُ ، لا بمجرَّدِ العقْلِ ، ولكنَّهُ بعثَ الرسلَ وأظهرَ صدقَهُمْ بالمعجزاتِ الظاهرةِ ، فبلَّغوا أمرَهُ ونهيَهُ ، ووعدَهُ ووعيدَهُ ، فوجبَ على الخلْقِ تصديقُهُمْ فيما جاءوا بهِ .

مَعْنَى الْكَلِمَةِ الثَّانِيَةِ ، وَهِيَ شَهَادَةُ الرَّسولِ صَلَّى اللهُ عَلَيهِ وَسَلَّمَ

وأنَّهُ بعثَ النبيَّ الأميَّ القرشيَّ مُحَمَّداً صلَّى اللهُ عليهِ وسلَّمَ برسالتِهِ إلى كافَّةِ العربِ والعجمِ ، والجنِّ والإنْسِ ، فنسخَ بشرعِهِ الشرائعَ إلا ما قرَّرَهُ منها ، وفضَّلَهُ على سائرِ الأنبياءِ ، وجعلَهُ سيِّدَ البشرِ ، ومنعَ كمالَ الإيمانِ بشهادةِ التوحيدِ ؛ وهوَ قوْلُ(لا إلهَ إلا اللهُ) ما لمْ تقترنْ بها شهادةُ الرسولِ ؛ وهوَ قولُكَ (مُحَمَّدٍ رَسُولُ اللهِ) .

وألزمَ الخلْقَ تصديقَهُ في جميعِ ما أخبرَ عنهُ منَ أمورِ الدنيا والآخرةِ ، وأنَّهُ لا يُتقبَّلُ إيمانُ عبدٍ حتَّىٰ يؤمنَ بما أخبرَ عنهُ بعدَ الموتِ ، وأوَّلُهُ سؤالُ مُنْكَرٍ ونَكِيرٍ ، وهما شخصانِ مهيبانِ هائلانِ ، يقعدانِ العبدَ في

in his grave in spirit and body. They will ask him about God's unity and His message, saying, "Who is your lord? What is your religion (*dīn*)? Who is your Prophet?" Their task is to conduct the trial of the grave, and their interrogation is the first of the trials that come after death.

It is obligatory to believe in the torment of the grave, and that it is true, wise, and just, and that it is meted out to the body and spirit according to [God's] will.

It is obligatory to believe in the balance (*mīzān*), which consists of two scales and a pointer (*lisān*); it is described as being as huge as the span between heaven and earth. Deeds are weighed in it by the power of God تَعَالَىٰ, and the weights placed on it that day will be as fine as a speck of dust or a mustard seed so that justice may be perfectly done. The pages recording good deeds will be placed in a beautiful form on the scale representing light, and the scale will be weighed down according to their rank in God's sight, by God's grace. Then the pages recording evil deeds will be placed in an ugly form on the scale representing darkness, countering the weight on the other side by God's justice.

It is obligatory to believe in the traverse (*ṣirāṭ*) stretching over the plain of hell. It is narrower than a sword's blade and finer than a hair. The feet of the disbelievers will slip on it by God's decree and they will fall into hell, while the feet of the believers will remain firm on it by God's grace, and they will be led into the abode of perpetuity.

It is obligatory to believe in the much-visited pool, the pool of Muḥammad صَلَّى ٱللَّهُ عَلَيْهِ وَسَلَّمَ from which the believers will drink before they enter paradise and after they cross over the traverse. Whoever drinks from it once will never be thirsty again. It is as broad as a month's journey, its water is whiter than milk and sweeter than honey. All around it are pitchers, as many as the stars in the sky. Two aqueducts pour into it from the [river of] Kawthar.

قبرِهِ سَوِيّاً ، ذا رُوحٍ وجسدٍ ، فيسألانِهِ عنِ التوحيدِ والرسالةِ ، ويقولانِ لهُ : مَنْ ربُّكَ ؟ وما دينُكَ ؟ ومَنْ نبيُّكَ ؟ وهما فتّانا القبرِ ، وسؤالُهُما أوَّلُ فتنةٍ بعدَ الموتِ .

وأنْ يؤمنَ بعذابِ القبرِ ، وأنَّهُ حَقٌّ وحكمةٌ وعَدْلٌ ، على الجسمِ والروحِ ، علىٰ ما يشاءُ .

وأنْ يُؤمنَ بالميزانِ ذي الكفَّتَينِ واللِّسانِ ، وصفَتُهُ في العظمِ أنَّهُ مثلُ طباقِ السمواتِ والأرضِ ، تُوزنُ فيهِ الأعمالُ بقدرةِ اللهِ تَعَالَىٰ ، والصَّنْجُ يومئذٍ مثاقيلُ الذرِّ والخردَلِ ؛ تحقيقاً لتمامِ العدلِ ، فتُطرحُ صحائفُ الحسناتِ في صورةٍ حسنةٍ في كفَّةِ النورِ ، فيثقلُ بها الميزانُ علىٰ قدْرِ درجاتِها عندَ اللهِ بفضْلِ اللهِ ، وتُطرحُ صحائفُ السيئاتِ في صورةٍ قبيحةٍ في كفَّةِ الظلمةِ ، فيخفُّ بها الميزانُ بعدْلِ اللهِ .

وأنْ يُؤمنَ بأنَّ الصراط حقٌّ ، وهوَ جسْرٌ ممدودٌ علىٰ متنِ جهنَّمَ ، أَحَدُّ منَ السيفِ ، وأدقُّ مِنَ الشعْرةِ ، تَزِلُّ عليهِ أقدامُ الكافرينَ بحكمِ اللهِ سبحانَهُ ، فتهوى بهِمْ إلى النارِ ، وتثبتُ عليهِ أقدامُ المؤمنينَ بفضلِ اللهِ ، فيُساقونَ إلىٰ دارِ القرارِ .

وأنْ يُؤمنَ بالحوضِ المورُودِ ، حوضِ مُحَمَّدٍ صَلَّى اللهُ عَلَيْهِ وَسَلَّمَ ، يشربُ منهُ المؤمنونَ قبلَ دخولِ الجنَّةِ وبعدَ جوازِ الصراطِ ، مَنْ شربَ منهُ شَربةً .. لمْ يظمأْ بعدَها أبداً ، عرضُهُ مسيرةُ شَهْرٍ ، ماؤُهُ أشدُّ بَيَاضاً مِنَ اللبنِ ، وأحلىٰ مِنَ العسلِ ، حولَهُ أباريقُ عددَ نجومِ السماءِ ، فيهِ ميزابانِ يصُبّانِ مِنَ الكوثَرِ .

It is obligatory to believe in the reckoning, and [to believe] that people therein will be dealt with in different ways, some called to account, others pardoned, and others, namely those who are nearest to God, admitted into paradise without any reckoning. God تَعَالَىٰ will ask some of the prophets about how they delivered their messages, and some of the disbelievers about how they belied the messengers عَلَيْهِمُ السَّلَامُ. He will ask the heretical innovators about the *sunna*, and the Muslims about their deeds.

It is obligatory to believe that all who believe in [God's] unity will be released from hell once they have paid for their sins until, by God's grace, not a single believer in [God's] unity will remain in hell. No one who believes in [God's] unity will remain in hell forever.

It is obligatory to believe in the intercession of the prophets, then [that of] the scholars, then the martyrs, then the rest of the believers, all of them according to his rank and standing before God تَعَالَىٰ. If any remaining believers without anyone to intercede for them, God عَزَّوَجَلَّ will take them out of hell by His own grace. No believer will remain in hell forever; even those with as little as an atom's weight of faith in their hearts will come out of it.

It is obligatory to believe in the virtue of the Companions رَضِيَ اللَّهُ عَنْهُمْ and their established ranks, and [to believe] that the best of people after the Messenger of God صَلَّى اللَّهُ عَلَيْهِ وَسَلَّمَ are Abū Bakr, then ʿUmar, then ʿUthmān, then ʿAlī رَضِيَ اللَّهُ عَنْهُمْ. One must think the best of all the Companions and praise them as God عَزَّوَجَلَّ and His Messenger صَلَّى اللَّهُ عَلَيْهِ وَسَلَّمَ praised them.

All of the foregoing has been related in reports [from the Prophet] and traditions [from the early Muslims]. To believe in all this with deep conviction is to be one of those who hold to the truth and follow the *sunna*, and [it is] to separate oneself from the people of misguidance and heretical innovation.

وأنْ يُؤمنَ بالحسابِ ، وتفاوتِ النَّاسِ فيهِ إلىٰ مناقَشٍ في الحسابِ وإلىٰ مسامحٍ فيهِ ، وإلىٰ مَنْ يدخلُ الجنَّةَ بغيرِ حسابٍ وهُمُ المقرَّبونَ ، فيسأَلُ اللهُ تَعَالَىٰ مَنْ شاءَ مِنَ الأنبياءِ عنْ تبليغِ الرسالَةِ ، ومَنْ شاءَ مِنَ الكفَّارِ عنْ تكذيبِ المرسلينَ ، ويسأَلُ المبتدعةَ عَنِ السنَّةِ ، ويسْأَلُ المسلمينَ عنِ الأعمالِ .

وأنْ يؤمِنَ بإخراجِ الموحِّدينَ مِنَ النارِ بعدَ الانتقامِ ، حتَّىٰ لا يَبقىٰ في جهنَّمَ موحِّدٌ بفضْلِ اللهِ تَعَالَىٰ ، فلا يخلدُ في النار موحِّدٌ .

وأنْ يؤمنَ بشفاعةِ الأنبياءِ ، ثمَّ العلماءِ ، ثمَّ الشهداءِ ، ثمَّ سائرِ المؤمنينَ ، كلٌّ علىٰ حَسَبِ جَاهِهِ ومنزلتِهِ عندَ اللهِ تَعَالَىٰ ، ومَنْ بقيَ مِنَ المؤمنينَ ولمْ يكنْ لهُ شفيعٌ . . أُخرجَ بفضْلِ اللهِ عَزَّ وَجَلَّ ، فلا يخلدُ في النارِ مؤمنٌ ، بلْ يخرُجُ منها مَنْ كانَ في قلبهِ مثقالُ ذرَّةٍ مِنَ الإيمانِ .

وأنْ يعتقِدَ فضْلَ الصحابةِ رضيَ اللهُ عنهُمْ ، وترتيبَهُمْ ، وأنَّ أفضلَ الناسِ بعد رسولِ اللهِ صَلَّى اللهُ عَلَيْهِ وَسَلَّمَ أبو بكرٍ ، ثمَّ عمرُ ، ثمَّ عثمانُ ، ثمَّ عليٌّ رَضِيَ اللهُ عَنْهُمْ ، وأنْ يُحسنَ الظنَّ بجميعِ الصحابةِ ، ويُثنيَ عليهِمْ كما أثنى اللهُ عَزَّ وَجَلَّ ورسولُهُ صَلَّى اللهُ عَلَيْهِ وَسَلَّمَ عليهِمْ أجمعينَ .

فكلُّ ذلكَ ممَّا وردتْ بِهِ الأخبارُ ، وشهدتْ بِهِ الآثارُ ، فمنِ اعتقدَ جميعَ ذلكَ موقناً بهِ . . كانَ مِنَ أهلِ الحقِّ وعصابةِ السنَّةِ ، وفارقَ رَهْطَ الضلالِ وحزْبَ البدعةِ .

We ask God تَعَالَىٰ, in His mercy, to grant us and all Muslims
perfect conviction and steadfastness in religion;
He is the most Merciful of the merciful.
May God bless our master
Muḥammad, and
every chosen
servant.

فنسألُ اللهَ تَعَالَىٰ كمالَ اليقينِ ، وحُسْنَ الثّبَاتِ فِي الدِّينِ ،
لنا ولكافَّةِ الْمُسْلِمِينَ برحمتِهِ ، إنَّهُ أرحمُ الراحمينَ ،
وَصَلَّى اللهُ عَلَى سَيِّدِنَا مُحَمَّدٍ
وَعَلَىٰ كُلِّ عَبْدٍ
مُصْطَفىً .

2

On Imparting Religious Instruction Gradually, and the Stages and Levels of Conviction

KNOW that what we said above in the exposition of creed should be presented to a child in his early years so that he can memorize it.[1] After that, its meaning should be revealed to him little by little as he grows. He begins with memorization, then understanding, then conviction, certitude, and belief in it. All this can be cultivated in the child without the need for rational arguments.

In His grace, God سُبْحَانَهُ opens the human heart to faith in its early stages of life without the need for rational proofs and arguments. How could this be denied, when the beliefs of the common folk are all based on simple instruction and solely on blind imitation?[2]

Of course, belief based on blind imitation will never be free of some kind of weakness in the beginning, in that it can be replaced by something contradictory if that is suggested instead. Therefore it must be strengthened and affirmed in the mind of the child and the common man until it is stable and unshakable.

The way to strengthen [their belief] and affirm it is not to teach the art of debate and theology; rather, it is to read the Qurʾān and its commentary, and the *ḥadīth* corpus and its interpretation, and to engage in regular acts of worship. By doing this, the conviction

1 "They should memorize it in their hearts well enough that they do not forget it and so that it takes root in their souls until it is like a stone [that has been] engraved and is not threatened by contradictory notions." Al-Zabīdī, *Itḥāf*, 2:42.

2 Other editions have "teaching" (*taʿlīm*) instead of "imitation" (*taqlīd*).

[of the common man] will continue to grow firmer as one hears the proofs and arguments of the Qurʾān, become familiar with the attestations and beneficial lessons of the *ḥadīth*, and receive the illuminations of regular acts of worship and devotion. They will further be strengthened by the benefits of seeing the righteous and sitting with them, experiencing their illuminated appearance, their words, and their comportment in being humble before God عَزَّوَجَلَّ, [being] fearful of Him, and [being] at peace with Him. Thus, the first instruction is like planting a seed in the heart, and then these other [aspects] serve to water and tend the seed until it grows and strengthens and becomes strong *like a good tree, whose root is firmly fixed, its branches* [*high*] *in the sky* [14:24].

Such a person must guard his ears to the fullest from debate and theology, because such debate will confuse him more than help him, and corrupt him more than benefit him. Indeed, trying to strengthen him with debate is like hitting a tree with an iron hammer hoping to strengthen it by making it firmer,[3] when [doing] this is far more likely to break it into pieces and destroy it. You can witness this with your own eyes, and that will be enough to explain it to you.

Compare the creed of righteous, pious common folk with the creed of theologians and debaters: you will see that the common man's belief is like a towering mountain, unmoved by calamities or lightning bolts, while the belief of the theologian who guards his creed with various rational arguments is like a thread blowing to and fro in the wind. The only exceptions to this are those of them who hear the rational proofs of [the] creed and blindly follow them just as they blindly followed the creed itself to begin with; for when it comes to blind following, there is no difference between learning the proof and learning the thing that it proves. Teaching the evidence is one thing, but deducing evidence through reflection is something very different.

Once the child has been raised on this creed, if he decides to follow an ordinary worldly life then nothing else will be opened up for him, but he will be safe in the hereafter because he holds to the creed of the people of truth. The law does not require any more from

3 Another edition has "making it larger."

the [ordinary] Arab people than firm belief in the outward import of these doctrines; as for delving into the details and producing a schema of rational proofs, they are not required to do this at all.

If [someone] decides that he wants to join the wayfarers on the path of the hereafter, and if granted success such that he engages in pious works, keeps to God-consciousness, restrains himself from desire, and busies himself with spiritual exercise and exertion—if he does this, then doors of guidance will open up for him and [they will] reveal the truths of this doctrine by means of a [divine] illumination cast into his heart because of his exertion and in honor of what God عَزَّوَجَلَّ promised when He said, *and those who strive for Us—We will surely guide them to Our ways* [29:69].

This is the precious pearl that is the utmost end of the faith of the veracious and those who are nearest to God. This is what was meant by the secret that was planted in the heart of Abū Bakr al-Ṣiddīq رَضِيَ ٱللَّهُ عَنْهُ, that gave him virtue above the rest of mankind.

Now the unveiling of this secret—or these secrets—has its own levels, commensurate with the levels of exertion and the levels of the inner being in its cleanness and purity from all besides God تَعَالَىٰ and its illumination with the light of certitude. This is no different from the disparity that exists between people in their knowledge of medicine, jurisprudence or any other science: this differs according to people's exertion as well as their natural gifts of intelligence and aptitude. Just as those levels are countless, so are these.[4]

Inquiry [on the Ruling on Studying Debate and Theology]

If you say: Is the study of debate and theology blameworthy like the study of astrology, or permitted, or recommended?

Answer: People have gone to different extremes in this matter. There are some who say that it is a heretical innovation, and forbidden, and that it would be better for a person to meet God عَزَّوَجَلَّ while

4 "The essence of what the author says here is that children and common folk should not be taught any more than the creed he summarized above, since it is enough to convince them and protect them from falling into harmful matters." Al-Zabīdī, *Itḥāf*, 2:46.

guilty of every sin except the attribution of partners to God, than [it would be] to meet Him while being guilty of [studying] theology. Others say that it is essential and obligatory, either for the Muslim community as a whole or for every individual Muslim, and that it is the best of deeds and the highest of devotions because it verifies the knowledge of the oneness of God and defends His religion.

Those who considered it forbidden included al-Shāfiʿī, Mālik, Aḥmad b. Ḥanbal, Sufyān, and all the people of *ḥadīth* among the early Muslims.

Ibn ʿAbd al-Aʿlā رَحِمَهُ ٱللَّهُ said,

> I heard al-Shāfiʿī رَضِيَ ٱللَّهُ عَنْهُ say on the day he debated Ḥafṣ al-Fard, a Muʿtazilī theologian, "It would be better for a man to meet God عَزَّ وَجَلَّ while guilty of every sin except attributing partners to Him than [it would be] to meet Him while guilty of any theology." I heard Ḥafṣ say things that I cannot repeat.[5]

He also said, "I heard things from the theologians that I had never even imagined. For a man to be tried by everything that God has forbidden except the attribution of partners to Him would be better for him than to study theology."[6]

Al-Karābīsī related that al-Shāfiʿī رَضِيَ ٱللَّهُ عَنْهُ was asked a question about theology, and became angry and said, "Ask Ḥafṣ al-Fard and his companions about it, may God disgrace them!"[7]

When al-Shāfiʿī رَضِيَ ٱللَّهُ عَنْهُ grew ill, Ḥafṣ al-Fard came to visit him and said, "Do you know who I am?"

He replied, "You are Ḥafṣ al-Fard—may God neither protect nor guide you until you repent from what you are doing."[8]

---

5 Ibn ʿAbd al-Barr, *Jāmiʿ bayān al-ʿilm wa-faḍlih*, 1788. The thing he declined to relate was his opinion that the Qurʾān is created.

6 Ibn ʿAbd al-Barr, *Jāmiʿ bayān al-ʿilm wa-faḍlih*, 1789.

7 Ibn ʿAbd al-Barr, *Jāmiʿ bayān al-ʿilm wa-faḍlih*, 1790.

8 Ibn ʿAbd al-Barr, *Jāmiʿ bayān al-ʿilm wa-faḍlih*, 1791. This is to show his displeasure and dissatisfaction at Ḥafṣ's actions, and not him as a person. The early Muslims truly believed that their actions, sayings, and beliefs represented something greater than their desires, curiosity, and learning. They believed that they had to hold themselves to higher standards and saw themselves as role models and guardians for future generations, just as the pious predecessors (*al-salaf al-ṣāliḥ*) of Muslims taught them through their teachings and actions. Therefore, he felt the need to verbalize his displeasure at Ḥafṣ's actions. Nevertheless, later genera-

He also said, "If the people knew the perils of the impulses [that result from delving into] theology, they would flee from it just as they flee from lions."[9]

He also said, "When you hear a man say, 'The name is identical with the named or distinct from the named,' recognize him as a man of theology with no religion."[10]

Al-Zaᶜfarānī related that al-Shāfiᶜī رضي الله عنه said, "My verdict on the theologians is that they be whipped with palm branches and paraded around the tribes and clans, accompanied by the herald: 'This is what will be done with those who renounce the Qurʾān and *sunna* and take up theology.'"[11]

Aḥmad b. Ḥanbal رحمه الله said, "The theologian will never prosper. It is rare to find any student of theology without some corruption in his heart."[12] [Aḥmad b. Ḥanbal] disdained it so much that he severed his friendship with al-Ḥārith al-Muḥāsibī, despite [al-Muḥāsibī's] asceticism and piety, because he wrote a book rebutting heretical innovators. Aḥmad رحمه الله said to him, "Woe unto you! Do you not relate their innovations first yourself, before rebutting them? By writing these things, do you not encourage people to read works of heresy and [do you not] engage their minds with these doubtful matters, thereby inspiring them to adopt these opinions and musings?"[13] Aḥmad رحمه الله also said, "The scholars of theology are heretics."[14]

Mālik رحمه الله said, "What would he do if someone more skilled at debating came to him—would he renounce his religion every day for a new one?" That is, the arguments of the debaters are always

---

tions of Muslims investigated these and many other theological issues in detail; an example of this is Fakhr al-Dīn al-Rāzī (d. 606/1210), who wrote volumes on this issue and defended Sunnī theology against many groups of his day, including the Muᶜtazila.

9 Ibn ᶜAbd al-Barr, *Jāmiᶜ bayān al-ᶜilm wa-faḍlih*, 1792.

10 Ibn ᶜAbd al-Barr, *Jāmiᶜ bayān al-ᶜilm wa-faḍlih*, 1792.

11 Ibn ᶜAbd al-Barr, *Jāmiᶜ bayān al-ᶜilm wa-faḍlih*, 1793.

12 Ibn ᶜAbd al-Barr, *Jāmiᶜ bayān al-ᶜilm wa-faḍlih*, 1796.

13 "Each of them were *imāms* of the first rank and guides for the Muslims. One ought to judge that al-Ḥārith spoke when it was necessary to speak, and that both of them were correct from a certain perspective. May God forgive them both." Al-Zabīdī, *Itḥāf*, 2:49.

14 Abū Ṭālib al-Makkī, *Qūt al-qulūb*, 1:138.

trumping one another.[15] Mālik رَحِمَهُ ٱللَّهُ also said, "The testimony of the people of heretical innovation and desires is not permissible." One of his companions explained this by saying, "By people of desires, he meant the theologians, whatever their school."[16]

Abū Yūsuf رَحِمَهُ ٱللَّهُ said, "Whoever seeks knowledge by means of theology will become a heretic."[17]

Ḥasan said, "Do not sit with people of desires, nor debate them, nor listen to their words."[18]

The people of *ḥadīth* among the early Muslims agreed on this point, and there are countless narrations of their stern condemnations of it. They said that the only reason the Companions were silent on it, although they had more knowledge of realities and more skill in expression than anyone, was that they knew of the evils that result from it. In this regard, the Prophet صَلَّى ٱللَّهُ عَلَيْهِ وَسَلَّمَ said, "Those who go too far will be ruined, those who go too far will be ruined, those who go too far will be ruined!"[19] That is, those who delve too deeply into intellectual investigations and inquiries.

They also argued that if theology were a rightful part of the religion, it would be the most important thing that the Messenger of God صَلَّى ٱللَّهُ عَلَيْهِ وَسَلَّمَ ever enjoined, and he would have taught the proper way to do it and praised it and those who mastered it. After all, he taught them how to clean themselves after answering calls of nature,[20] and encouraged them to learn the laws of estate division and praised them for doing so.[21] Yet he discouraged them from speaking about predestination and said, "Be silent."[22]

The Companions رَضِيَ ٱللَّهُ عَنْهُمْ continued to adhere to this. To go above one's teacher is impertinent and unjust, and they are our teachers and role models, while we are their students and followers.

---

15 Al-Lālikāʾī, *Sharḥ uṣūl iʿtiqād ahl al-sunna*, 1:144. "It means that these arguments should not be relied on because they can always be replaced by stronger arguments." Al-Zabīdī, *Itḥāf*, 2:49.

16 Ibn ʿAbd al-Barr, *Jāmiʿ bayān al-ʿilm wa-faḍlih*, 1800.

17 Abū Ṭālib al-Makkī, *Qūt al-qulūb*, 1:139.

18 Al-Dārimī, *Sunan*, 415 and Ibn ʿAbd al-Barr, *Jāmiʿ bayān al-ʿilm wa-faḍlih*, 1803.

19 Muslim, 2670.

20 As in Muslim, 262.

21 As in al-Tirmidhī, 2091; Ibn Māja, 2719.

22 Al-Ṭabarānī, *al-Muʿjam al-kabīr*, 2:96; and Abū Nuʿaym, *Ḥilya*, 4:108.

The other side argued that if theology is blameworthy because of technical terms like "substance," "essence," and other unusual terms that the Companions رَضِيَ ٱللَّهُ عَنْهُمْ did not use, then it is not the only [science] that does this, for there is not a single science for which technical terms have not been devised to aid understanding. This is true of the sciences of *ḥadīth*, Qurʾānic commentary, and jurisprudence. If the Companions were presented with technical terms like *naqḍ* [false analogy], *kasr* [false equivalence], *tarkīb* [compositional analogy], *taʿdiya* [transition of premise], *fasād al-waḍʿ* [false application] and other such issues relating to legal analogy, they would not understand them. Inventing new technical terms to refer to concepts correctly is no different than inventing a new kind of container in which to store lawful items.

If [they say], on the other hand, [that] theology is blameworthy because of its meaning, then we intend nothing by it but recognition of the proofs that the world is contingent, the Creator is One, and His attributes are those described by revelation. Why should it be forbidden to recognize God تَعَالَىٰ through rational proofs?

And if theology is blameworthy because of the argumentation, partisanship, enmity, and anger that it can lead to, then all this is forbidden and must be avoided. Likewise, the study of *ḥadīth*, Qurʾānic interpretation, and jurisprudence can lead to arrogance, pride, ostentation, and ambition, all of which are forbidden and must be avoided; yet we do not say that these sciences are forbidden because of their possible consequences. How could discussing, seeking, and studying rational arguments be blameworthy when God تَعَالَىٰ says, *Say: produce your proof* [2:111], and says, *that those who perished [through disbelief] would perish upon evidence and those who lived [in faith] would live upon evidence* [8:42], and says, *You have no authority for this [claim]* [10:68]; that is, any proof or rational argument (*burhān*). And He says, *With God is the far-reaching argument* [6:149] and says, *Have you not considered the one who argued with Abraham about his Lord … So the disbeliever was overwhelmed [by astonishment]* [2:258]; in that verse, He سُبْحَانَهُ speaks in praiseworthy terms of how Abraham defeated his rival through argument and debate. He تَعَالَىٰ also says, *And that was Our [conclusive] argument* (ḥujja) *which We gave Abraham against his people* [6:83], and says, *They said, "O*

Noah, you have disputed [with] us and been frequent in disputing with us" [11:32]. In the story of Pharaoh, He تَعَالَىٰ tells us how he said, *And what is the Lord of the worlds* [26:23], up to His words, *Even if I brought you proof manifest?* [26:30].

In sum, the Qurʾān from beginning to end is a debate with the disbelievers. The theologians base their proofs for [God's] unity on His تَعَالَىٰ words, *Had there been in the heavens and earth gods besides God, they both would have been ruined* [21:22], their proofs for prophethood on His words, *And if you are in doubt about what We have sent down upon Our servant [Muḥammad], then produce a sura the like thereof* [2:23], and their proofs for the resurrection on His تَعَالَىٰ words, *Say, "He will give them life who produced them the first time"* [36:79]. There are many other examples like these.

The messengers عَلَيْهِمُ السَّلَامُ continued to argue and debate with those who belied them. God says, *argue with them in a way that is best* [16:125]. The Companions رَضِيَ اللَّهُ عَنْهُمْ also argued and debated with [those who] denied [*tawḥīd*], but only when necessary, and there was little need for it in their time.

The first one to establish the practice of inviting heretics back to the truth by means of debate was ʿAlī b. Abī Ṭālib رَضِيَ اللَّهُ عَنْهُ when he sent Ibn ʿAbbās رَضِيَ اللَّهُ عَنْهُمَا to speak to the Khawārij.[23]

He said, "What fault do you find with your *imām*?"

They said, "He fought but did not take captives or booty."

He said, "That [i.e., taking captives or booty] is only done when fighting against disbelievers. Tell me—had ʿĀʾisha رَضِيَ اللَّهُ عَنْهَا been taken captive at the battle of the camel and been given to one of you in your share, would you have treated her like a common slave, when the Qurʾān itself calls her your mother?"[24]

---

23 According to al-Sharastānī: "Anyone who opposed (*kharaj*) the true leader (*imām*) that the majority (*jamaʿa*) had agreed upon is called a Kharajī (pl. Khawārij), regardless of when the act of opposition takes place, whether it was in the time of the Companions of the Messenger, [during the period of the] rightly guided-*imāms* or after them, during the time of those who followed them [during the period of any] *imām* at any time." *al-Milal wa-niḥal*, 132. Historically Khawārij refers to the group that opposed ʿAlī b. Abū Ṭālib at the battle of Ṣiffīn; it specifically refers to al-ʿAshath b. Qays al-Kindī, Musʿr b. Fadkī al-Tamīmī, and Zayd b. Ḥaṣīn al-Ṭaʾī.

24 The Khawārij considered ʿAlī b. Abī Ṭālib رَضِيَ اللَّهُ عَنْهُ a heretic, and their proof for this was that he did not take any booty at the battle of the camel. Ibn ʿAbbās رَضِيَ اللَّهُ عَنْهُمَا

They said no, and some two thousand of them gave up their rebellion because of his argument.[25]

It is related that Ḥasan debated a member of the Qadariyya[26] sect and succeeded in convincing him to renounce his heresy. ʿAlī b. Abī Ṭālib (may God ennoble his face) himself debated a member of the Qadariyya sect.

ʿAbdallāh b. Masʿūd رَضِوَاللَّهُ عَنْهُ debated Yazīd b. ʿAmīra about faith.

ʿAbdallāh رَضِوَاللَّهُ عَنْهُ said, "To say 'I am a believer' is to say 'I shall be in paradise.'"

Yazīd b. ʿAmīra said, "O Companion of the Messenger of God صَلَّىٰٱللَّهُعَلَيْهِوَسَلَّمَ, this is an error on your part. Faith is to believe in God and His angels, books, and messengers, and in the resurrection and the reckoning, and to pray, fast, and give the *zakāt*. We are guilty of sins, and only if we knew them to be forgiven could we say that we are people of paradise. Because of this, we say that we are believers, not that we are people of paradise."

Ibn Masʿūd رَضِوَاللَّهُ عَنْهُ said, "You are right, by God, and I was in the wrong."[27]

It remains to be said that they would engage in [debate] only rarely and briefly, not frequently and at length. They would do it when the need arose, and did not compose works on it, teach it or make a vocation of it. It has been said that the reason they engaged in it only rarely was that there was little need for it because heresy (*bidʿa*) had not yet become widespread at that time.

As for their brevity, it was because the goal was to silence their interlocutor and teach him, disclose the truth, and remove doubts;

---

asked, how could he have taken captives when ʿĀʾisha رَضِوَاللَّهُ عَنْهَا (the mother of the believers and the wife of the Prophet) would have been among those they would have taken captive. Had she been taken captive, it would have been a violation of the clear Qurʾānic ruling that the Prophet's wives are to be treated as the mothers of the believers and therefore could not be taken captive in a battle. So the basis of declaring ʿAlī b. Abī Ṭālib رَضِوَاللَّهُ عَنْهُ a heretic was invalid.

25 Ibn ʿAbd al-Barr, *Jāmiʿ bayān al-ʿilm wa faḍlih*, 1834, abridged. Also given by Abū Nuʿaym, *Ḥilya*, 1:318.

26 The Qadarīs believed in unfettered free will and did not believe in the Muslim concept of predestination. The Muʿtazila adopted the Qadarī doctrine as one of their basic tenants.

27 See Ibn ʿAsākir, *Tārīkh Dimashq*, 11:461.

if he had many doubts or objections, there is no doubt that they would have continued the discussion for as long as necessary. They did not calculate the need with a weight or measure, as it were, after beginning the discussion.

As for the fact that they did not undertake teaching [theology] or compose works on it, the same applies to jurisprudence, interpretation, and *ḥadīth*. If it is permitted to write works of jurisprudence and discuss hypothetical situations that occur only rarely in reality, whether by way of preparation for their potential albeit unlikely occurrence, or simply as an intellectual exercise, then we must also be permitted to organize the methods of argumentation in preparation for when they are needed, such as when a doubt arises or a heretic emerges, or else simply as an intellectual exercise, or to store the argument in the mind so that when it is needed it can be retrieved quickly and without delay, just as weapons are prepared in peacetime for the day when war comes. This is all that can be said about the two sides of this issue.

❁ ❁ ❁

Now, if you ask which side I take I would say the truth is that it is a mistake to say it is blameworthy at all times or that it is praiseworthy at all times. Rather, a distinction should be made.

First, know that something can be forbidden in and of itself, such as wine or carrion. By "in and of itself," I mean that the reason it is forbidden is because of something intrinsic to itself, namely, in these cases, intoxication and death. If we were asked about one of these things, we would say without qualification that they are forbidden. Let us not muddy the waters now with the consideration that carrion is lawful in times of dire need, or that it is permitted to drink wine if one is choking and has nothing else to remove the object lodged in the throat.[28]

28 "This seems to be the answer to an unspoken question, i.e., 'How can it be said without qualification that they are forbidden, when they are both permitted at certain times?' So he answered that these are rare exceptions that prove the rule." Al-Zabīdī, *Itḥāf*, 2:57.

Other things are forbidden because of something extraneous to them, such as selling something you have already promised to sell to your fellow Muslim during the period when there is still an option to cancel, or selling [something] during the call to prayer [on Friday], or eating soil, which is forbidden because of its harmful effects.

This is then divided into two categories: there are those things that cause harm in both large and small amounts, in which case they are ruled to be unlawful; an example is any poison that kills in both large and small doses. Then there are those things that do harm in large amounts only, in which case they are ruled to be lawful; an example is honey, which is harmful to a feverish person when taken in large doses. Another example is eating soil. So when clay and wine are ruled to be forbidden while honey is ruled to be lawful, this ruling is based on the usual state of things. When something new comes along that has different effects in different situations, the best and safest thing to do is to treat each situation independently.

Returning to the subject of theology, we can say that it has both potential benefits and potential harms. In those situations where it is beneficial, it is ruled permitted, recommended, or even obligatory, depending on the situation. In those times and places where it is harmful, it is ruled forbidden.

The potential harms [of theology] are that it can raise doubts and unsettle convictions, which [then] no longer rest on a firm and resolute foundation. This is something that happens at the beginning, and there is no guarantee that what has been lost can be won back with rational proofs, for it differs from person to person. These are its potential harms to true belief.

Another potential harm of [theology] is [that it] strengthens heretics in their heretical belief and makes their hearts more at ease with it, so that they are more encouraged to preach it and insist on it. However, this harm is the result of the partisan zealotry that comes from debate; this is why you see that the common man from a heretical sect can be very quickly won over with kind words, unless he is from a place where argument and partisan zealotry are very common, in which case even if everyone in the world joined together to remove the heresy from his heart, they would be unable to do it. Desire, partisanship, and hatred for his rivals and opponents overwhelm his heart and prevent him from seeing the truth, to the point that if he were asked, "Would you like God تَعَالَىٰ to remove the veil for you and show you firsthand that your rival is in the right?" he would refuse this in fear that his rival would rejoice in his defeat. This is the fatal disease that spreads through the land and the people. It is a kind of corruption caused by those who engage in partisan debate.[29] These are the potential harms of theology.

Now as for its potential benefits, one might imagine that its benefit is that it unveils realities and allows them to be known as they really are—but this is far from the truth. Theology does not provide the means for attaining that noble goal, and perhaps it confuses and misguides more than it reveals and teaches. If you hear this from a scholar of *ḥadīth* or an extreme literalist, you might imagine that it is simply a case of people hating what they do not know; so hear it instead from one well-versed in theology, [one] who renounced it after gaining mastery of it, [one who] immersed himself in it to the furthest extent any theologian ever could, then fathomed the depths of other sciences that are forms of theology, and then realized for certain that the path to the realities of gnosis is closed from that direction [i.e., the direction of theology].

Upon my word, the most that theology can do is to disclose and shed light on certain limited matters, and then only rarely; and these matters are obvious things that could almost be understood without delving into the art of theology at all. Indeed, it has one benefit only: to protect the creed of the common folk as we outlined it above, and to guard [the creed] from the misgivings of heretics by means of different kinds of argumentation. The common man is weak and can be unsettled by a heretic's arguments, even if he is corrupt; and fighting one corrupt thing with another can dispel it. People are required to hold to the creed we have outlined, the law has enjoined it because of how it benefits them in their religious and worldly lives, and the righteous early Muslims have agreed on

29 See al-Ghazālī, *al-Iqtiṣād fī l-iʿtiqād*, 77, Eng. trans., 12.

it. The scholars are required to protect this creed for the common folk from the confusion of heretics, just as the ruler is required to protect their property from the attacks of invaders and thieves.

Now that its benefits and harms have been enumerated, one must be like a skilled doctor in how he uses dangerous medicine, [he must] only prescribe it when appropriate: at the required time, and in the required amount.

By way of further specification: common folk engaged in trades and skills ought to be left alone with the sound doctrines in which they believe, as long as they have been taught the correct creed we outlined above. Teaching them theology would be nothing but harmful for them, as it might instill doubts in them and cause their conviction to waver in such a way that cannot be rectified.

As for the common man who has heretical beliefs, he must be invited back to the truth with kindness, not partisan rigor, and with kind words that convince the soul and move the heart, with citations from the Qurʾān and *ḥadīth* mixed with skillful counsel and admonition. This is more beneficial than arguing in the style of the theologians, for if the common man hears that, he will think that it is mere rhetorical trickery that the theologian has learned in order to fool people into accepting his beliefs; and even if he is unable to answer it himself, he will assume that the theologians of his own school would be able to.

It is forbidden to debate with either of these two, or with anyone who develops doubt about something; his doubt should be removed with kind words and counsel and simple evidence that he can accept, [one must] stay away from the depths of theology.

Argumentation can be beneficial in one circumstance only, namely when a common man adopts a heretical belief after hearing some kind of argument, in which case this argument should be countered with another of the same kind so that he returns to true belief. This only applies when the person is by nature attracted to debate and so cannot be swayed by ordinary counsel and admonitions. Such a person has ended up in a condition where the only cure is argumentation, and so it is permitted to give it to him.

This applies in lands where heresy is rare and there are not many different schools of thought. In such places, no more is needed than the creed we have outlined, and no rational proofs are required unless a doubt arises, whereupon they should be administered as needed.

Now in lands where heresy is widespread and even children are at risk of being deceived, there is no harm in teaching them theology at the level of our book *al-Risāla al-qudsiyya*.[30] This will protect them from the effects of any heretical arguments that might come their way. It is a brief treatise, and we have included in it this book because of its brevity.

If an intelligent person is led by his intelligence to a particular question, or doubt arises in his mind, this means that a dangerous malady has appeared and an ailment has come to light, and there is no harm in treating it by moving him up to the level of our book *al-Iqtiṣād fī l-iʿtiqād*, which consists of about fifty folios and does not stray from the topic of the principles of creed to any other areas of interest for the theologians.

If this convinces him, then that is the end of it. If it does not, this means that the illness has become chronic, the disease critical, and the sickness grave, and the doctor must treat him as carefully as he can and wait for God's decree for him, until the truth is revealed to him by God Himself. Otherwise, the doubt and uncertainty will continue for as long as it is destined to.

The content of that book and other books on its level is likely to be beneficial. As for the fields that lie outside of its content, they are of two kinds:

THE FIRST KIND is the study of things extraneous to the principles of creed, such as propensities, generations,[31] perceptions, and questions such as whether vision has an opposite called "obstruction" or "blindness," and if that opposite does exist, whether it is one single obstruction of all visible things, or whether every visible thing has an obstruction of its own, and other misleading trivialities.

---

30 *Al-Risāla al-qudsiyya* ("The Jerusalem Epistle"), chapter 3 of this book, serves as a commentary on the creed.

31 "Propensity (*iʿtimād*) is a term used by such figures as Abū Hāshim, who said, when discussing causality, that an object takes its weight from its propensity, and not from motion. Generation (*kawn*, pl. *akwān*) means a substance has a positive qualitative change, as opposed to degeneration or corruption (*fasād*). The word is also used in other senses." Al-Zabīdī, *Itḥāf*, 2:61.

The second kind is the expansion of these rational proofs beyond the realm of those principles, and the addition of more questions and answers. This is also an endeavor that adds nothing but misguidance and ignorance to the one who is not convinced by the previous amount [of proofs, questions, and answers]; for some discourse increases the perplexity of [the issue] and makes it more obscure.

Now someone might say that studying the nature of perceptions and propensities is beneficial because it sharpens the mind, and the mind is the tool of the religion just as the sword is the tool [with which one] strives in the way of God. Therefore there is no harm in sharpening it. This is like saying that playing chess sharpens the mind and therefore must be a religious [practice], which is absurd. The mind can be sharpened by other sciences of Islam that do not pose similar risks.

You have now acquainted yourself with the praiseworthy and blameworthy sides of theology, the situations in which it is either praiseworthy or blameworthy, and the types of people who can or cannot benefit from it.

❁ ❁ ❁

Now you might say, "Since you have acknowledged that it is necessary to dispel heresy, and in these times many heresies have arisen, tribulations are widespread, and the need is overbearing, then instruction in this science ought to be viewed as a communal obligation (*farḍ kifāya*) akin to the protection of property and other rights by means of the legal and state systems, and so on. If scholars do not work to disseminate, teach, and study it, it will not last; and if it is neglected entirely, it will disappear. Human nature does not have the power to resist the doubts raised by heretics unless it is taught [theology], and therefore its teaching ought also to be viewed as a communal obligation. This was not true at the time of the Companions رَضِيَ ٱللَّهُ عَنْهُمْ, because there was no pressing need for it."

Know, then, that the truth is that every land ought to have people who engage in this science and undertake to rebuff the doubts raised by heretics who arise in those lands. With this, the teaching of it will persist. However, it is not correct to teach it comprehensively in the way that jurisprudence or interpretation are taught, for it is like medicine, while jurisprudence is like food: food is not especially likely to be harmful, while medicine is highly likely to be so, because of all the potential harms we outlined earlier.

The scholar of theology should teach this science only to those who have three attributes:

The first is that they be solely devoted to study and have no worldly occupation, for those with professions will be too busy to complete their studies and eliminate any doubts that might arise.

The second is that they have intelligence, sagacity, and eloquence, because an unintelligent person will not benefit from any understanding, and a dull-witted person will not benefit from any argument. Such people are more likely to be harmed by theology than to benefit from it.

The third is that they be naturally righteous, religious, and pious and that they not be governed by desires (*shahawāt*).[32] A wicked person will renounce faith at the slightest doubt, for this frees him of all restrictions and removes for him the barrier between him and all sorts of pleasure. He will not work to remove any doubts in his mind, but indeed will encourage them so that he can free himself from the shackles of [religious] responsibility. Thus studying theology will corrupt him more than it rectifies him.

Now that you have become acquainted with these details, you can clearly see that the kind of theological argumentation that is praiseworthy is that composed of Qurʾānic arguments in the form of kind words that move the heart and convince the soul, without delving into details and subtleties that most people cannot understand; and if they did understand them, they would think them to be tricks and artifices employed by the theologian for the purpose of deception, and [they would think] that [these tricks] could be rebuffed by any other trickster of similar skill.

32 "Here 'desires' means zealous partisanship to any school of thought and the desire to boast about one's knowledge." Al-Zabīdī, *Itḥāf*, 2:63.

Recognize that al-Shāfiʿī and the early Muslims only forbade delving into this science and devoting oneself to its study because of the potential harms in it that we have outlined. Also recognize that the examples we cited of Ibn ʿAbbās رَضِيَ ٱللَّهُ عَنْهُمَا debating the Khawārij and ʿAlī رَضِيَ ٱللَّهُ عَنْهُ debating the Qadariyya, and so on, were clear and obvious theological arguments and were employed in a time of need; and this is always praiseworthy. It is clearly true that the need for it differs from era to era, and therefore it is by no means outlandish to suggest that the ruling on it might differ in the same way.

This is the judgment concerning this creed, according to which humanity should worship, and [this is] the ruling on the right way to protect and preserve it. As for removing doubts, disclosing realities, gaining cognition of things as they truly are, and gleaning the secrets symbolized by the outward language of this creed, the only way to unlock this is through spiritual striving, fighting against one's desires, turning one's whole being toward God تَعَالَىٰ, and maintaining pure concentrated thought free of the turbidities of arguments. This is a mercy from God عَزَّوَجَلَّ that is granted to those who expose themselves to the breezes that bear it, commensurate with their provisions and their efforts as well as their aptitude and the purity of their hearts. This is an ocean whose depths cannot be fathomed, nor its shores reached.

Inquiry [Is There an Outward Creed and an Inward Creed?]

These words seem to suggest that these sciences have outward appearances and inward mysteries, and that while some of them are obvious and can be understood at first sight, others are subtle and can only be made clear by spiritual striving, discipline, earnest seeking, pure thought, and an innermost being free of all worldly concerns and fixed on the goal. Now this would appear to be contrary to the law, for the law does not have outward and inward aspects, nor open and mysterious aspects; rather, the outward, inward, open, and mysterious are all the same.

Answer: No person of true insight would deny the division of these sciences into categories of subtle and obvious; rather, this is only denied by the ignorant who, having been taught things in their youth and [having] adhered rigidly to them, did not advance to anything higher, nor to the stations of the scholars and saints. The law itself provides clear proof that this distinction does exist.

The Prophet صَلَّى ٱللَّهُ عَلَيْهِ وَسَلَّمَ said, "The Qurʾān has an outward and an inward, a boundary and a horizon."[33]

ʿAlī رَضِيَ ٱللَّهُ عَنْهُ said, pointing to his breast, "There is abundant knowledge gathered here; if only I had found someone to bear it!"[34]

The Prophet صَلَّى ٱللَّهُ عَلَيْهِ وَسَلَّمَ said, "We prophets have been commanded to speak to people according to the capacity of their minds."[35]

He صَلَّى ٱللَّهُ عَلَيْهِ وَسَلَّمَ also said, "Whenever someone tells people something their minds cannot comprehend, it brings tribulation upon them."[36]

---

33 Ibn Ḥibbān, *Ṣaḥīḥ*, 74, with the wording, "The Qurʾān was revealed in seven modes, each verse of it having an inward and an outward." ʿAbd al-Razzāq, *al-Muṣannaf*, 3:358, as a saying of Ḥasan with the wording, "By Him in whose hand is my soul, every verse in it has an inward and an outward, and every letter has a boundary, and every boundary has a horizon." The wording given by al-Ghazālī here is cited in Abū Ṭālib al-Makkī, *Qūt al-qulūb*, 1:51, with the author commenting, "Its outward is for the people of the Arabic language, its inward for the people of certitude, its boundary for the literalists, and its horizon for the people of eminence, namely the gnostics, who love and fear [God]. They discovered the subtleties of the horizon after fearing its awesome power, and then they stowed that secret in a secure place, and gained mastery over the text. Thus they drew near to Him by virtue of their witness of Him; the Prophet صَلَّى ٱللَّهُ عَلَيْهِ وَسَلَّمَ said, 'The witness sees what the absent man does not.' He who is present witnesses; he who witnesses experiences; he who experiences unifies; he who unifies glorifies. Likewise, he who is absent is blind; he who is blind loses; he who loses forgets; he who forgets is forgotten. God عَزَّ وَجَلَّ says, *Thus did Our signs come to you, and you forgot them; and thus will you this Day be forgotten* (20:126). That is, you ignored them and did not take heed of them nor look upon them, and so today you will be ignored, neither looked upon with mercy, nor addressed with kindness, nor brought nearer in comfort."

34 Abū Nuʿaym, *Ḥilya*, 1:79–80 and al-Khaṭīb al-Baghdādī, *Tārīkh Baghdād*, 6:376. See also Abū Ṭālib al-Makkī, *Qūt al-qulūb*, 1:142–143, and al-Zabīdī, *Itḥāf*, 1:406.

35 Al-ʿUqaylī, *al-Ḍuʿafāʾ*, 4:1534, with a similar wording; it resembles in meaning the previously cited *ḥadīth* of al-Bukhārī ,127, where it is given as a saying of ʿAlī b. Abū Ṭālib رَضِيَ ٱللَّهُ عَنْهُ as: "Speak to the people in a way they can understand…"

36 Al-ʿUqaylī, *al-Ḍuʿafāʾ*, 3:937, on ʿAbdallāh b. ʿAbbās رَضِيَ ٱللَّهُ عَنْهُمَا authority as a *ḥadīth* and by Muslim in the introduction as a saying of ʿAbdallāh b. Masʿūd رَضِيَ ٱللَّهُ عَنْهُ.

God تَعَالَىٰ says, *And these examples We present to the people, but none will understand them except those of knowledge* [29:43].

The Prophet صَلَّىٱللَّهُعَلَيْهِوَسَلَّمَ said, "Some knowledge is, as it were, hidden, known only to those who have knowledge of God..." to the end of the *ḥadīth*,[37] as we gave it in the *Kitāb al-ʿilm* [*The Book of Knowledge*].

He صَلَّىٱللَّهُعَلَيْهِوَسَلَّمَ also said, "If you knew what I know, you would laugh little and weep much."[38] Upon my word, if this were not a mystery that could not be divulged because some minds could not understand it, or for some other reason, then why did he not mention it to them?[39] They would certainly have believed it had he told them.

Ibn ʿAbbās رَضِيَٱللَّهُعَنْهُمَا said about God's عَزَّوَجَلَّ words, *It is God who has created seven heavens and of the earth, the like of them. [His] command descends among them* [65:12], "Were I to tell you what this means, you would stone me to death." Another version records that he said, "You would call me a disbeliever."[40]

Abū Hurayra رَضِيَٱللَّهُعَنْهُ said, "I have treasured in my memory two stores of knowledge from the Messenger of God صَلَّىٱللَّهُعَلَيْهِوَسَلَّمَ. One I have divulged, but were I to divulge the other you would cut my throat."[41]

The Prophet صَلَّىٱللَّهُعَلَيْهِوَسَلَّمَ said, "Abū Bakr did not surpass you because of much fasting and praying, but because of a mystery that resides in his heart."[42] There is no doubt that this mystery pertained to the principles of the religion and not to anything outside them;

---

37 Abū Ṭālib al-Makkī, *Qūt al-qulūb*, 1:175, with missing narrators. Al-Mundhirī said in *al-Targhīb wa-l-tarhīb*, 1:135, that it was reported by al-Daylamī, *Musnad*, 802, and by al-Sulamī in *al-Arbaʿīn*, which is his work on Sufism.

38 Al-Bukhārī, 1044 and Muslim, 426.

39 That is, this is a mystery that cannot be divulged because some minds cannot understand it—and so the Prophet did not mention it. It is something that is beyond the ability of man's faculties to comprehend.

40 Ibn al-Ḍarīs, *Faḍāʾil al-Qurʾān*, 3, and al-Ṭabarī, *Tafsīr*, 14:188, with a similar wording. It is quoted with this wording in Abū Ṭālib al-Makkī, *Qūt al-qulūb*, 1:253.

41 al-Bukhārī, 120.

42 Aḥmad b. Ḥanbal, *Faḍāʾil al-ṣaḥāba*, 118, Abū Dāwūd, *al-Zuhd*, 37, and al-Ḥakīm al-Tirmidhī, *Nawādir al-uṣūl*, 31, and al-Ḥakīm al-Tirmidhī, *Khatam al-awliyāʾ*, 442, as a saying of Bakr b. ʿAbdallāh al-Muzanī.

and no outward aspect of the principles of the religion was beyond the knowledge of anyone else.[43]

Sahl al-Tustarī رَضِيَ ٱللَّهُ عَنْهُ said, "The scholar may possess three kinds of knowledge: outward knowledge, which he imparts to the people concerned with the exoteric; esoteric knowledge, which he can only divulge to those who are qualified for it; and knowledge that is between him and God تَعَالَىٰ, which he divulges to no one."[44]

A gnostic said, "To divulge the secret of lordship is an act of disbelief (*kufr*)."[45]

Another of them said, "Lordship has a secret that, if revealed, would do away with prophethood. Prophethood has a mystery that, if divulged, would do away with knowledge. Those who know God have a mystery that, if they revealed it, would do away with all laws."[46]

Now unless this person meant that prophethood would be done away with in the case of the weak because of their imperfect understanding, then what he said is not true, for the truth is that there need not be any contradiction: the perfect man is the one whose light of gnosis does not extinguish the light of his piety, and prophethood is the font of all piety.

Inquiry [on the Difference Between the Outward and the Inward]

THESE [Qurʾānic] verses and reports can be interpreted in many ways, to show us how the inward and outward differ. If the inward contradicts the outward, this amounts to doing away with the law, like those who say that the reality (*ḥaqīqa*) is opposed to the law (*sharīʿa*), which amounts to disbelief, because the law means the outward while the reality means the inward. If, on the other hand, the one does not contradict or oppose the other, this means

---

43 That is, among the Companions. Al-Zabīdī, *Itḥāf*, 2:68.

44 Abū Ṭālib al-Makkī, *Qūt al-qulūb*, 2:90.

45 Abū Ṭālib al-Makkī, *Qūt al-qulūb*, 2:90. Al-Ghazālī explains what this means in *al-Imlāʾ*, 31.

46 Abū Ṭālib al-Makkī, *Qūt al-qulūb*, 2:90. Al-Ghazālī comments on it in *al-Imlāʾ*, 39, and attributes it to Sahl al-Tustarī.

that they are the same thing, and that the division does not exist, and that the law does not have an unrevealed mystery; rather, the hidden and the obvious are one and the same.

Answer: This question raises a momentous issue and leads us into the sciences of unveiling (*mukāshafa*) and away from the sciences of practical conduct (*muʿāmala*), which are the subject of these books. The creed we have outlined is the acts of the heart, and we are required to receive it with acceptance and belief by attaching the heart to it, not by seeking to have its realities disclosed to us, which is not a task that every human being has been charged with. Were it not a kind of [religious] act, we would not have mentioned it in this book at all; and were it not an outward action of the heart rather than an inward one, we would not have mentioned it in the first half of the book. True unveiling is an attribute of the innermost being and core of the heart. However, since in the natural flow of this discussion we have reached the problem of the perceived contradiction between the outward and the inward, we must briefly touch on how to solve this problem.

Those who say that the reality opposes the law, or that the inward contradicts the outward, are nearer to disbelief than to faith.[47] The truth is that there are mysteries that only those nearest to God can perceive, while most people cannot share in this knowledge and those who have it do not divulge it to them. These mysteries may be divided into five categories [as below].

The first category [includes] things that, by their nature, are subtle and beyond the reach of most minds, so that the elite are naturally the only ones who can perceive them. They must not divulge them to those who are not qualified for it; that would only bring them tribulation because their minds would fall short of understanding them. One example of this is the nature of the spirit, which is a mystery that the Prophet himself صَلَّىٰ ٱللَّٰهُ عَلَيْهِ وَسَلَّمَ declined to divulge.[48] Its reality is something that minds cannot comprehend, nor can imaginations conceive of its nature.

47 See al-Ghazālī, *Mishkāt al-anwār*, 61.

48 Al-Bukhārī, 125, and Muslim, 2794.

But do not imagine that this was not unveiled to the Messenger of God صَلَّى ٱللَّٰهُ عَلَيْهِ وَسَلَّمَ; for the one who does not know the spirit cannot truly know himself—and how then could he know his Lord?

Nor is it far-fetched [to think] that this could have been unveiled to some saints and scholars even if they were not prophets; they follow the conduct of the law and keep silent on all that the law keeps silent on.[49] Indeed, there are many hidden aspects of the attributes of God عَزَّ وَجَلَّ that cannot be understood by all people, and the Messenger of God صَلَّى ٱللَّٰهُ عَلَيْهِ وَسَلَّمَ only spoke of those that minds can easily comprehend, such as knowledge, power, and so on, so that people understood them by referring to their own knowledge and power: they have attributes of their own that are called "knowledge" and "power," so they based their understanding of [God's attributes] on this. Had he told them about [God's] attributes for which there are no reference points in the attributes of men, they would not have understood it. If you were to describe sexual pleasure to a child or impotent man, he would only be able to understand it by making reference to his experience of the pleasure of eating food, and this would not be anything like a true understanding. The difference between the knowledge and power of God and the knowledge and power of human beings is greater than the difference between the pleasures of sex and food.

In sum, a man can perceive only his own self and his own attributes as they exist at the present moment or as they existed in the past; and then by comparing them to himself, he can understand others, after which he might acknowledge that there is a difference between them in nobility and perfection. All a human being can do is affirm for God the same attributes that he affirms for himself, such as action, knowledge, power, and so on, while acknowledging that [in God] they are more perfect and noble. Thus his emphasis will mostly be on his own attributes, not on those that belong only to the Lord in His majesty. This is why the Messenger of God صَلَّى ٱللَّٰهُ عَلَيْهِ وَسَلَّمَ said, "I cannot praise You enough; You are as You have praised

49 "There is no issue more in dispute among the scholars of transmitted knowledge and rational inquiry (*al-ʿaql wa-l-naql*) than that of the nature of the spirit. It would be better for people to know their limits and accept their weaknesses." Al-Zabīdī, *Itḥāf*, 2:70.

Yourself."[50] This does not mean "I am unable to express what I have perceived"; rather it is a confession of the inability to perceive the true nature of His majesty.

This is why someone said that no one can truly know God but God Himself عَزَّوَجَلَّ. And [Abū Bakr] al-Ṣiddīq رَضِيَ ٱللَّهُ عَنْهُ said, "Praise be to God, who has not given mankind any way to know Him except to acknowledge that they cannot know Him."[51]

Let us not digress any further, but return to our subject here, which is that one of these five categories is that which minds are unable to comprehend; these things include the nature of the spirit and the attributes of God تَعَالَىٰ. It may be to these things that the Prophet صَلَّى ٱللَّهُ عَلَيْهِ وَسَلَّمَ was alluding when he said, "God سُبْحَانَهُ has seventy veils of light. Were He to draw them back, the rays of His countenance would burn everything upon which His sight fell."[52]

❖ ❖ ❖

THE SECOND CATEGORY of hidden things that the prophets and veracious ones are not allowed to divulge is that which can be understood in itself without causing the mind problems, but it damages most of those who hear it, though it does not damage the prophets and veracious ones. One example of this is the mystery of predestination, which those who know it are forbidden to divulge to all. It is not far-fetched that certain truths should be harmful to some people, just as sunlight is harmful to the eyes of a bat, or the fragrance of a rose is harmful to dung beetles.

How should it not be harmful, for we say, "Disbelief, adultery, sin, and evil all take place by God's decree, will, and volition." This is completely true in itself, yet it has harmed many people to hear this because they took it as an invitation to recklessness, abandonment

---

50 Muslim, 486.

51 al-Qushayrī, *al-Risāla al-Qushayriyya*, 495.

52 Muslim, 179, with the wording "His veil is light," and with "seventy veils" by al-Ṭabarānī, *al-Muʿjam al-awsaṭ*, 6403.

of wisdom, and contentment with vileness and evil. Ibn al-Rāwandī and many unfortunate folk were led into outright disbelief by this.[53]

Likewise, if the secret of predestination were divulged, it would make most people suspect some kind of defect, for their minds would be unable to perceive anything to remove this suspicion.

Furthermore, one might say that if the date of the resurrection were to be divulged as being after a thousand years, or more, or less, this communication would be perfectly understandable. However, its date has not been given for the good of humankind and to avoid harm; for if the time for it were far off in the future, complacency would increase. And when people think the time of punishment is delayed, they become indifferent. On the other hand, God سُبْحَانَهُ might know it to be near, and if this were divulged there would be mass hysteria and people would neglect their daily work, and the world would fall into chaos. If this argument is also sound and apt, it can also be counted as an example of this category.

The third category is that which can be understood without causing any harm if stated plainly, but is usually alluded to with euphemisms and symbolic language so that it has a more profound impact on the heart. The value of this is that it makes a greater impression on the heart. For example, a man may say, "I saw so-and-so hanging pearls around the necks of swine," [thus] using this to symbolize the divulgence of knowledge and wisdom to an unworthy recipient. The common man who hears this will call to mind the literal image depicted by the words, while the person of acumen will perceive that this person did not really have any pearls, nor was he near any pigs, and will therefore uncover the mystery and inner meaning. People have different degrees in this regard. Another example is found in the poet's words:

53 Abū l-Ḥusayn b. Isḥāq al-Rāwandī (d. 910) was a Muʿtazilī theologian who became a heretic and bitter critic of religion. See Ibn al-Nadīm, *The Fihrist of al-Nadīm*, trans. Dodge, 1:419–423.

Two men, a tailor and a weaver,
Face each other beyond the Spica:[54]

One weaving shrouds for the departed,
The other sewing swaddling for new arrivals.

Here, [the poet uses the] symbolism of a heavenly cause for the arrival and departure [of souls].

This category centers on the expression of concepts using images that either comprise the concept or symbolize it. Another example is found in the Prophet's ﷺ words, "A mosque shrinks when people spit in it just as skin shrinks from fire."[55] You know full well that the courtyard of the mosque does not really shrink when people spit in it; what it means is that the spirit of the mosque should be venerated, and spitting in it is disrespectful, for it is contrary to the status of a mosque just as fire is contrary to being in contact with the layers of the skin.

Another example is found in the Prophet's ﷺ words, "Does the one who raises his head before the *imām* not fear that God will turn his head into the head of a donkey?"[56] From the perspective of the actual form, this has never happened and it never will, but from the perspective of meaning, it does occur because the defining attribute of the donkey's head is not found in its color or shape, but in what it symbolizes, namely foolishness and stupidity. The one who raises his head before the *imām* has made his head like a donkey's head in the sense of foolishness and stupidity, and this is what is meant, not the shape, which is only the material form that houses the symbolic meaning. It is the height of stupidity to seek to follow and lead at the same time, for they are opposites.

Now the way to know if this secret is meant figuratively rather than literally is to follow the indicators of either intelligence or the law. In the case of intelligence, it can be known by realizing

54 Spica Virginis (*al-simāk al-aʿzal*) is a star in the constellation of Virgo which can be occulted by the moon. There are two stars called *simāk*, Spica and Arcturus (*al-simāk al-rāmiḥ*). Al-Zabīdī, *Itḥāf*, 2:75.

55 ʿAbd al-Razzaq, *al-Muṣannaf*, 1:433; and Ibn Abī Shayba, *al-Muṣannaf*, 7550, as a saying of Abū Hurayra.

56 Al-Bukhārī, 691; and Muslim, 427.

that a literal interpretation is not possible, as in the case of the Prophet's ﷺ words, "The believer's heart is between two of the fingers of the All-Compassionate."[57] If we examine the hearts of the believers, we find no fingers on them, and therefore we know that these words are meant to symbolize [God's] omnipotence, which is the secret and hidden spirit of these "fingers." The reason fingers were chosen as symbols of [God's] omnipotence is that they convey in the best way the understanding of complete omnipotence.

Another example of words symbolizing [God's] omnipotence can be found in God's words *Our word to a thing, when We intend it, is but that We say to it, "Be!" and it is* [16:40]. This cannot be taken literally, because to say "Be!" to something before that thing even existed would be impossible, because the non-existent thing could not understand the words in order to obey them; nor could the command be issued after the thing had come into being, since then the command would serve no purpose, being already fulfilled. However, since this way of expressing things has a greater impact on the soul in [terms of] conveying what [God's] omnipotence is, He employs it.

As for the guidance of the law, it applies when a passage could be interpreted literally but is talked about as having a figurative meaning. An example of this is the narration about the interpretation of God's words *He sends down from the sky, rain/water, and valleys flow according to their capacity, and the torrent carries a rising foam* [13:17], stating that the "water" symbolizes the Qurʾān and the "valleys" [symbolize] hearts, some of which bear a lot, others a little, and others none at all. Then the foam symbolizes disbelief and hypocrisy which, when they rise and float on the surface of the "water," do not remain, while the guidance that benefits mankind does remain.

Some have gone too far with this kind of interpretation, making figurative interpretations of certain narrations about the hereafter such as the balance, the traverse, and so on. This is a heretical innovation because there are no narrations affirming these interpretations and it is not impossible [i.e., it is possible] to take these things literally, and therefore they must be taken literally.

---

57 Muslim, 2654, with a slightly different wording.

The fourth category is to perceive something in general terms, and then to perceive it in detail through realization and taste so that it becomes a state that he experiences firsthand. These two types of knowledge are hierarchical: the first is like the husk, the second like the kernel. The first is like the outer appearance, the second like the inner reality. It is as when a person sees another person in the dark or from a distance, so that he gains some sort of knowledge about him; and then when he sees him up close or in the light, he finds a difference between the two visions. The second does not oppose the first, but rather completes it.

The same is true of knowledge, faith, and belief: a person might believe in the existence of passionate love (*ʿishq*), sickness, and death before they occur, but when they occur he realizes them in a more perfect way than he did before they occurred. Indeed, when it comes to desire, passionate love, and other states, there are three hierarchical states and distinct perceptions: The first is to believe in something before it happens, the second is to believe in it when it happens, and the third is to believe in it after it has ended. Your realization of hunger after it ends is not the same as your realization of it before it ends.

In the same way, some religious knowledge becomes perfected when it is experienced, and this is like the inner reality of what was there before this. There is a difference between the sick person's knowledge of health and the healthy person's knowledge of it.

So people have differing levels in these four categories. In every one of them, the inward does not contradict the outward but rather completes and perfects it just as the kernel completes the husk. That is that.

❁ ❁ ❁

The fifth category is when concrete words are used to express abstract concepts. The person with limited understanding goes no further than the outward meaning of the words, while the person of deep insight, on the other hand, perceives the secret within it. An example: "The wall said to the chisel, 'Why are you splitting me?' The chisel replied, 'Ask the one who is hitting me, for he will not let me go. Look to the hammer behind me.'" This is a concrete expression of an abstract concept.

Another example of this can be found in God's words, *Then He directed Himself to the heaven while it was smoke and said to it and to the earth, "Come* [*into being*], *willingly or by compulsion." They said, "We have come willingly"* [41:11]. A dull-witted person can only understand this by imagining that heaven and earth are endowed with life, intelligence, and understanding, and that audible words were spoken to them, which they heard and to which they responded with voices of their own, saying, "We have come willingly." The person of insight, on the other hand, knows that this is a figure of speech meant to show that heaven and earth are naturally and innately subservient [to God's will].

Another example can be found in God's words *And there is not a thing except that it exalts* [*God*] *by His praise but you do not understand their* [*way of*] *exalting* [17:44]. The dull-witted person can only understand this by imagining that an inanimate object is endowed with life, intelligence, and audible speech to allow it to say, "Glory be to God," in order to realize its glorification. The person of insight, on the other hand, knows that this does not mean the speech of the tongue, but rather that this object glorifies [God] by its existence, declares [God's] holiness by its essence, and attests to His Oneness, as the poet said:

> In everything there is a sign,
> Showing that He is One.[58]

When it is said, "This masterpiece attests to the wonderful skill and extensive knowledge of its maker," this does not mean that the masterpiece literally says, "I attest to this," but rather that its essence and state are proof of this. Likewise, everything that exists is in need of something to bring it into existence and sustain it, and to maintain its attributes and move it through its different states. Through this need, it attests to the holiness of its Creator, and its testimony is perceived by the people of insight but not by those who

58 Abū l-ʿAtāhiyya, 104.

go no further than outward appearances. This is why God says, *But you do not understand their [way of] exalting* [17:44].

Those of limited understanding do not understand it at all, while those nearest to God and those of sound knowledge do not understand its nature and its perfection. All things attest in different ways to the holiness of God سُبْحَانَهُ and His glorification, and everyone perceives this according to the capacity of his intellect and insight. Yet to enumerate those attestations would be beyond the scope of our present study of conduct.

In this field, again, the people of literal meanings and the people of insight have hierarchical levels of knowledge, and the difference between the outward and the inward can be seen clearly in it.

Now in this station, people either go to extremes or follow the way of moderation. Some of those who went to extremes went so far in opposing literalism as to discard all literal meanings and external proofs, to the extent that they claimed figurative interpretations for God's words, *their hands will speak to Us, and their feet will testify about what they used to earn* [36:65], His words, *And they will say to their skins, "Why have you testified against us?" They will say, "We were made to speak by God, who has made everything speak"* [41:21], the dialogues of Munkar and Nakīr, the balance, the reckoning, and the dialogues between the denizens of paradise and hell when they say, *Pour upon us some water, or from whatever God has provided you* [7:50].[59]

Others went to extremes in closing the door to figurative interpretation, [these] include Aḥmad b. Ḥanbal, who even forbade a figurative interpretation of God's words *"Be!" and it is*. They claimed that this is actually spoken with audible words that God عَزَّوَجَلَّ speaks in every moment to everything that exists. I have even heard one adherent of his school say that [Aḥmad b. Ḥanbal رَحِمَهُ ٱللَّهُ] forbade figurative interpretation of all but three things: the Prophet's صَلَّى ٱللَّهُ عَلَيْهِ وَسَلَّمَ words "The black stone is God's

59 This refers to all those who rule by reason and put it before revelation, specifically those philosophers who went to extremes and denied the bodily resurrection; in another sense it refers to the Muʿtazila, as the author explains.

right hand on earth,"[60] his words "The believer's heart is between two of the fingers of the All-Compassionate,"[61] and his words, "I can feel the breath of the All-Compassionate blowing from Yemen."[62] The literalists also inclined toward closing the door on figurative interpretation altogether.

Now I believe that Aḥmad b. Ḥanbal رَحِمَهُ ٱللَّهُ knew that God's "ascendancy" [over His throne] does not mean that He literally sits on it, and that God's "descent" does not mean that He literally moves. Nevertheless, he forbade figurative interpretation in order to close the door and look after the common interest, for he deemed that if the door were opened, people would go too far and things would get out of hand, and the way of moderation would be transgressed, given how difficult it is to determine just what the way of moderation is.[63] There is nothing wrong with this approach, and the actions of the early Muslims attest to it, for they used to say, "Let them be just as they are."[64] Mālik رَحِمَهُ ٱللَّهُ even said, when asked about God's "ascendancy" over the throne, "The ascendancy is known, but its modality is unknown. Faith in it is obligatory, and asking about it is a heretical innovation."[65]

Others chose to follow the way of moderation and opened the door to figurative interpretation for everything regarding the attributes of God تَعَالَىٰ, while still taking the narrations about the

---

60 Al-Ḥākim al-Nīsābūrī, *al-Mustadrak*, 1:457; and al-Ṭabarānī, *al-Muʿjam al-awsaṭ*, 567, on the authority of ʿAbdallāh b. ʿAmr and by ʿAbd al-Razzāq, *al-Muṣannaf*, 5:39, as a saying of ʿAbdallāh b. ʿAbbās.

61 Muslim, 2654.

62 Al-Ṭabarānī, *al-Muʿjam al-kabīr*, 7:52; and Aḥmad b. Ḥanbal, *Musnad*, 2:540, with "your Lord" instead of "the Compassionate."

63 Al-Ghazālī composed his short but valuable treatise, *Qānūn al-taʾwīl*, to address this need.

64 Ḥasan b. Ismāʿīl al-Ḍarrāb narrated in *Manāqib Mālik* that al-Walīd b. Muslim said, "I asked Mālik, al-Awzāʿī, Sufyān, and Layth about these *ḥadīth*s that speak of vision, image, and descent, and they all said, 'Relate them just as they are.'" Al-Zabīdī, *Itḥāf*, 2:80.

65 Al-Lālakāʾī, *Sharḥ uṣūl iʿtiqād ahl al-sunna*, 3:397, from Umm Salama رَضِيَ ٱللَّهُ عَنْهَا. He then mentions the statement of Mālik رَحِمَهُ ٱللَّهُ. The different narrations of it are given in al-Suyūṭī, *al-Durr al-manthūr*, 3:473; and al-Zabīdī, *Itḥāf*, 2:80.

hereafter literally and forbidding any figurative interpretation of them. These are the Ashʿarīs.[66]

The Muʿtazila[67] went even further, making figurative interpretations of some of God's attributes like vision,[68] hearing, and sight. They also interpreted the ascension [of the Prophet] figuratively, claiming that it was not physical. They did the same with the punishment of the grave, the balance, the traverse, and several other matters of the hereafter. However, they did accept that the resurrection will be physical and that heaven is a real place containing foods, perfumes, conjugal relations, and other sensory pleasures, and that the fire is a real place where bodies are physically burned, skins split, and fat melted.

The philosophers went further still, making figurative interpretations for everything reported about the hereafter and saying that the suffering is psychological and spiritual, and the pleasures are intellectual. They denied physical resurrection and said that only souls survive, and that they are then punished or rewarded with intangible suffering or bliss. They are the ones who went too far.

The way of moderation between this excessively liberal approach and the stubborn literalism of the Ḥanbalīs is subtle and difficult to pin down. None find it except those granted success [from God], those who perceive things with illumination [from God] rather than only by transmitted reports. Then, when the mysteries of things as they truly are, are unveiled to them, they go back to the traditions and narrations, and affirm what accords with what they have witnessed with the light of certitude, and figuratively interpret what does not accord with it. As for the one who takes the cognition of these things from transmitted reports alone, he will not be able to secure a firm foothold in them or find a solid position. It is better

---

66 The Ashʿarīs (who make up the majority of Sunnī Muslims) follow the creed and theological teachings of Abū l-Ḥasan al-Ashʿarī (d. 324/935 or 936).

67 The Muʿtazilīs followed a rationalist Sunnī school of theology that rose to prominence during the ʿAbbāsid period.They maintained an extreme view of God's justice that limited His acts and they insisted on the createdness of the Qurʾān, which they considered sacrosanct.

68 This refers to the belief that the people of paradise will see God.

for those who confine themselves to transmitted reports alone to take the position of Aḥmad b. Ḥanbal رَحِمَهُ ٱللَّهُ.

Now to disclose the proper way of moderation in these matters would require us to delve into the science of unveiling, and to speak on it at length, which we shall not do here. Our only aim was to explain how the inner meaning accords with the outward and how it differs from it, and our examination of these five categories has achieved this end.

We consider the creed we outlined above sufficient for the needs of the common folk, who need not be burdened with any more than that at the first level. However, when there is risk of confusion because of prevalent heresy, it is necessary to move on to the second level of the creed, which contains glimpses of brief rational evidences, without going into too much depth.

Therefore, let us provide these glimpses in this book, limiting ourselves to what we outlined for the people of Jerusalem and entitled "The Jerusalem Epistle on the Principles of the Creed," which will constitute the third chapter of this book.

3

Shining Proofs of the Creed, Entitled "The Jerusalem Epistle on the Principles of the Creed" (*al-Risāla al-qudsiyya fī qawāʿid al-ʿaqāʾid*)

In the Name of God, the All-Merciful, the All-Compassionate

PRAISE be to God, who distinguished the partisans of the *sunna* with the illuminations of certitude, and favored the people of truth by guiding them to the buttresses of the religion; who kept them clear of the errors of the errant and the misguidance of the apostates, and graced them with success in following the guidance of the master of messengers and emulating his noble Companions; who enabled them to walk in the footsteps of the righteous predecessors, so that they were protected from the requirements of rational inquiries by holding fast to the firmest rope, and [they were] kept from repeating the mistakes of the previous communities in their creeds by remaining on the clear path. In this, they reconciled the consequences of rational inquiries with the pronouncements of the transmitted law, and realized that expressing the devotional testimony "There is no god but God" is pointless and without benefit unless one completely comprehends the pillars and principles related to this testimony. They recognized that the two testimonies, despite their brevity, contain an affirmation of [God's] essence, attributes, and acts, and an affirmation of the veracity of the Messenger. Thus they came to know that faith is centered on these four pillars, each of which is centered on ten foundations.

The first pillar is recognition of God's تَعَالَىٰ essence. It has ten foundations: knowledge of God's سُبْحَانَهُ existence, beginninglessness, and endlessness; knowledge that He is not a substance, body, or accident; knowledge that He سُبْحَانَهُ is not in any direction nor resident in any place, and that He can be seen, and that He is One.

The second pillar concerns His سُبْحَانَهُ attributes, and has ten foundations: knowledge that He is living (*ḥayyān*), knowing (*ʿālimān*), all-powerful (*qādirān*), volitional (*muridān*), hearing (*samīʿān*), seeing (*baṣīrān*), speaking (*mutakalimān*); that He is transcendently beyond being incarnate in any contingent thing;[1] and that His speech (*kalām*), knowledge (*ʿilm*), and will (*irāda*) are beginningless (*qadīm*).

The third pillar concerns His تَعَالَىٰ acts, and has ten foundations: that human actions are created by God تَعَالَىٰ, and that they are acquired by people, and that they are willed by God تَعَالَىٰ; that He creates and originates freely through His grace; that He is able to charge [people] with more than they could bear; that He is able to cause the innocent to suffer; that He is not obliged to do what is most beneficial; that only the law can impose obligations; that it is [rationally] possible for Him to send prophets; and that the prophethood of Muḥammad صَلَّىٰ ٱللَّهُ عَلَيْهِ وَسَلَّمَ is affirmed and supported by miracles.

The fourth pillar pertains to things known by transmitted reports, and has ten foundations: to affirm the resurrection and reckoning, the punishment of the grave, the questions of Munkar and Nakīr, the balance, the traverse (*ṣirāṭ*), the creation of paradise (*janna*) and the fire, the rulings pertaining to the *imām*, the virtues of the Companions in their hierarchical order, the conditions of the *imāma*, and [to affirm] that even if a potential *imām* does not possess piety and knowledge, his rule is valid if he fulfills the other conditions.

---

1 The words "transcendently beyond being incarnate in any contingent thing" are not counted as part of the ten foundations because technically it is one of the negative attributes (*al-ṣifāt al-salbiyya*).

The First Pillar of Faith:
Recognition of the Essence of God, and that God is One

This pillar has ten foundations.

THE FIRST FOUNDATION is recognition of God's existence. The first source of light to illuminate this, and the first path to follow to reflect on this, is the guidance provided by the Qurʾān; for no explanation is better than that offered by God Himself. God تَعَالَىٰ says: *Have We not made the earth a resting place? And the mountains as stakes? And We created you in pairs, and made your sleep [a means for] rest, and made the night as clothing, and made the day for livelihood, and constructed above you seven strong [heavens], and made [therein] a burning lamp, and sent down, from the rain clouds, pouring water, that We may bring forth thereby grain and vegetation, and gardens of entwined growth?* [78:6–16].

And again, *Indeed, in the creation of the heavens and earth, and the alternation of the night and the day, and the [great] ships which sail through the sea with that which benefits people, and what God has sent down from the heavens of rain, giving life thereby to the earth after its lifelessness and dispersing therein every [kind of] moving creature, and [His] directing of the winds and the clouds controlled between the heaven and the earth are signs for a people who use reason* [2:164].

And again, *Do you not consider how God has created seven heavens in layers, and made the moon therein a [reflected] light and made the sun a burning lamp? And God has caused you to grow from the earth a [progressive] growth, then He will return you into it and extract you [another] extraction* [71:15–18].

And again, *Have you seen that which you emit? Is it you who creates it, or are We the Creator? We have decreed death among you, and We are not to be outdone. In that We will change your likenesses and produce you in that [form] which you do not know. And you have already known the first creation, so will you not remember? And have you seen that [seed] which you sow? Is it you who makes it grow, or are We the grower? If We willed, We could make it [dry] debris, and you would remain in wonder, [Saying], "Indeed, we are [now] in debt; rather, we have been deprived." And have you seen the water that you drink? Is it you who brought it down from the clouds, or is it*

We who bring it down? If We willed, We could make it bitter, so why are you not grateful? And have you seen the fire that you ignite? Is it you who produced its tree, or are We the producer? We have made it a reminder and provision for the travelers [56:58–73].

Anyone with the least intelligence who reflects even briefly on the content of these verses and looks toward the wonders of God's creation on earth and in the heavens, and the amazing nature of animals and plants, will not fail to see that such wondrous things and such wise order must have a maker to arrange them and a power to govern and measure them. Indeed, human nature itself testifies that it is subject to His will and bent to His governance. For this reason God تَعَالَىٰ says, *Can there be doubt about God, Creator of the heavens and earth?* [14:10].

Therefore the prophets عَلَيْهِمُ ٱلسَّلَامُ were sent to call humanity to [God's] unity, that they might say, "There is no god but God." They were not commanded to say, "We have a God and the world has a God," because this was naturally inherent in their minds from the time of their childhood and the prime of [their] youth. This is why God says, *And if you asked them, "Who created the heavens and earth?" they would surely say, "God." Say, "[All] praise is [due] to God"* [31:25], and again, *So direct your face toward the religion, inclining to truth. [Adhere to] the fiṭra of God upon which He has created [all] people. No change should there be in the creation of God. That is the correct religion, but most of the people do not know* [30:30].

So there is in human nature and the attestations of the Qurʾān that which is sufficient to establish proof. However, for the sake of clarity and emulation of the insightful scholars, we say: It is among the self-evident truths of the intellects that all contingent things need a cause to bring them into existence. The world is contingent, and therefore it must have a cause.

As for our claim that all contingent things need a cause, it is obvious because every contingent thing exists at a particular time and the mind can imagine it coming earlier or later; it therefore follows that for it to exist at that particular time, and not at a later or earlier one, it requires, of necessity, that which particularizes it. As for our claim that the world is contingent, the proof of it is that the bodies that make up the world are always either in motion or at rest, and these are both contingent states; and anything that is never independent of contingencies must itself be contingent. Now this proof involves three claims:

THE FIRST [CLAIM] is that bodies are always either in motion or at rest. This is comprehended as self-evident and necessary and requires no meditation or thought. Anyone who thinks that a body can be neither at rest nor in motion is simply ignorant and devoid of intelligence.

THE SECOND CLAIM is that motion and rest are contingent states. This is proven by how they succeed each other and [because] the existence of one of the two occurs after the other. This is attested to by all bodies, both those that have been observed and those that have not. The mind knows that every object at rest could potentially move, and that every object in motion could potentially come to rest. When one of these states begins, it must be contingent because it has a beginning, and the preceding state must be contingent because it is now non-existent. For if its eternality were confirmed, it would be impossible for it to be non-existent. We shall explain and prove this when we come to the affirmation of the exalted and sanctified Creator's endlessness.

THE THIRD CLAIM is that anything that is never independent of contingencies must itself be contingent. The proof of this is that were it not so, every contingent thing would be preceded by an infinite chain of contingent things; and if that chain of contingent things had no end, there would be no termination of alternating occurrences that lead to the present contingent thing that exists at this moment, for the completion of that which has no end is impossible.

Another proof is found in the orbits of the celestial bodies: if they were eternal, their number would have to be either even or odd, or even and odd simultaneously, or neither even nor odd. It is impossible that they could be even and odd simultaneously, or neither even nor odd, for this would be a simultaneous negation and affirmation, yet in the affirmation of one of them is negation of the other, and in the negation of one of them is the affirmation of the other. It is also impossible that they could be even, since an even number becomes odd when one is added to it; and how could an infinite number be in need of one? Likewise, it is impossible that they could be odd, because an odd number becomes even when one is added to it; and how could one be lacking from them, when their number is infinite?[2]

The upshot of this is that the world is never independent of contingencies, and anything that is never independent of contingencies must itself be contingent. Since it is established that it is contingent, its need for an originator is among those [concepts] comprehended by necessity.

THE SECOND FOUNDATION is the knowledge that the Maker تَعَالَىٰ is beginningless and eternal without there being any beginning to His existence, and moreover that He is prior to each thing and precedes all life and death.

The proof of this is that if He were contingent, He would not be eternal (*qadīm*), and would Himself require an originator, and His originator would require an originator, and this would go on in an infinite regress, which is absurd. Either that, or it would go back to an eternal originator, who would be the first; and that is precisely what we are discussing now, and what we call the Creator of the world, its Maker, Originator, and Initiator.[3]

THE THIRD FOUNDATION is knowledge that God تَعَالَىٰ, while being beginningless (*azalī*), is also endless (*abadī*), there being no finality to His existence. *He is the First and the Last, the Outward and the Inward* [57:3] because that which is confirmed to be eternal cannot be non-existent.

The proof of this is that if He could ever cease to exist, this could only be either by Him bringing an end to Himself, or a rival power bringing an end to Him. If it were possible for a thing whose perpetuity is conceivable to become non-existent, it would also be

---

2 See al-Ghazālī, *al-Iqtiṣād,* 99, Eng. trans., 37–38 and al-Ghazālī, *Tahāfut al-falāsifa,* 99, Eng. trans., 19, for a refutation of those who claim that the infinite cannot be described as even and odd.

3 Al-Ghazālī says in *al-Iqtiṣād,* 102, Eng. trans., 41, "By 'beginningless' (*qadīm*), we mean that His being was not preceded by non-being. The word 'beginningless' (*qadīm*) does no more than affirm a being and negate a prior non-being; do not imagine that beginninglessness (*qadam*) is a concept added to the essence of the beginningless being (*al-qadīm*), such that you would have to say that this concept is also beginningless (*qadīm*) with its own added beginninglessness (*qadam*), and so on ad infinitum."

possible for a thing whose non-existence is conceivable to come into being; for just as a sudden emergence into being requires a cause, a sudden disappearance into non-being also requires a cause.

It is a falsity that He can become non-existent by a rival power that causes the non-existence because that which caused non-existence, were it eternal, would not be conceived as having an existent alongside it.[4] Now, His existence and eternality have been established by the two previous principles, so how could one conceive of any rival sharing in His eternal existence?

It is likewise impossible for the rival who causes non-existence to be a contingent entity, since the contingent entity, given its opposition to the eternal entity, would eliminate [the eternal entity's] existence, [and the contingent entity] is not in a superior condition relative to the eternal entity, given [that the contingent entity's] opposition to the eternal entity would prevent [the eternal entity] from becoming existent. Rather, the prevention would be easier than the destruction, and the eternal entity would be superior to the contingent one.

The fourth foundation is knowledge that God تَعَالَىٰ is not a substance that occupies space, but rather He is exalted and holy beyond any association with space. The proof of this is that every substance that occupies space is conditioned by this space, and must either remain at rest inside it, or move out of it. Thus it must be either in motion or at rest, which are both contingent states, and anything that is never independent of contingencies must itself be contingent. But were it possible to conceive of an eternal substance occupying a space, it would be possible to conceive of the substances of the world being eternal.[5] Now were someone to call Him a substance but not intend thereby that He occupies a space, they would be incorrect with regard to the word, but not [with regard to] the meaning.[6]

The fifth foundation is knowledge that God تَعَالَىٰ is not a body composed of substances. The word "body" means something

4 "That is, the Creator would not be able to coexist with that rival power in the first place, because absolute opposites cannot coexist." Al-Zabīdī, *Itḥāf*, 2:98.

5 This is false and inconceivable because substance is a possibility, and possibilities cannot be eternal because they require a being to bring them into existence.

6 See al-Ghazālī, *al-Iqtiṣād*, 107, Eng. trans., 45–46.

composed of substances, and given that we have established that He is not a substance that occupies space, He cannot be a body. All bodies occupy space and are composed of substances added together, and it is impossible for them to be independent of separation and conjunction, motion and rest, and form and quantity, all of which are characteristics of contingent beings. Were it valid to believe that the Creator of the world is a body, it would be equally valid to believe in the divinity of the sun, the moon, or any other kind of body. Now if anyone were to dare to call Him تَعَالَىٰ a body without meaning that He is composed of substances, they would be incorrect with regard to the word, but at the same time correct in negating the corporeal meaning of the word.

THE SIXTH FOUNDATION is knowledge that God تَعَالَىٰ is not an accident inherent in a body or located in a locus. The proof of this is that an accident must have a body for its locus, and all bodies are undoubtedly contingent while the originator must exist prior to it. How, then, could He be located in a body, when He existed before time began when there was no one but Him, after which He brought all bodies and accidents into being? Besides, He is All-Knowing, Omnipotent, Volitional, and [the] Creator, as will be shown, and it is impossible for an accident to have these attributes; indeed, they are not conceivable for any but a self-sustained existent that is independent in its essence.

These foundations show that He is a self-sustaining being and not a substance, body, or accident, while the whole universe is composed of substances, accidents, and bodies. Therefore He does not resemble anything, nor does anything resemble Him. He is the Living, the Self-Existing (*al-qayyūm*), and *there is nothing like unto Him* [42:11].[7] How could the creation resemble its Creator, the predestined being its Determiner, or the fashioned being its Fashioner? All bodies and accidents are of His creation and production. One cannot rightly deem it possible for them to be like Him or resemble Him.

THE SEVENTH FOUNDATION is knowledge that God تَعَالَىٰ transcends being specified by direction. Direction means either up or down, right or left, front or back. These are the directions that were created

---

7 "These foundations, namely the fourth, fifth, and sixth, show that He تَعَالَىٰ is unlike all contingent beings, and [He is] self-existing." Al-Zabīdī, *Itḥāf*, 2:101.

and originated through the creation of a person: He created him with two extremities, one resting on earth [that is] called the foot, and the other at the opposite end called the head. Thus the word "up" was assigned to that which corresponds to the head, and "down" to that which corresponds to the feet. This applies even to an ant crawling upside down on the ceiling: what is down in relation to [the ant] is up in relation to us.

He also created man with two hands, one of which is usually stronger than the other. Thus the word "right" was assigned to the stronger one, and "left" to the other, and then the direction by the right hand was called right, and the one by the left hand called left. He also created him with two sides, from one of which he sees and moves toward [something]. Thus the word "front" was assigned to the direction toward which he moves, and the word "back" to the other direction.

The directions, then, are contingent upon the creation of the person. Had people not been created in this form, but instead created spherical like a ball, these directions would not exist at all. How, then, could [God], in the state of beginninglessness, have been specified by direction, when direction is contingent? Or how could He have become specified by direction after it emerged from non-being?

Did He create the world above Himself? Far be it that anything could be above Him, for He is exalted above having a head, and the notion of "up" [or "above"] refers to what is in the direction of the head. Or did He create the world below Himself? Far be it that anything could be below Him, for He is exalted above having feet, and the notion of "down" [or "below"] refers to what is in the direction of the feet. All of this is rationally impossible.

Moreover, to conceive of His being specified by a direction would require the assumption that He occupies space in the way that substances do, or occupies a substance in the way accidents do. We have seen that it is impossible for Him to be a substance or an accident. Therefore it is impossible that He is specified by direction. Again, if the word "direction" is used to mean something other than these two concepts, it would be a mistake with regard to the word, but possibly helpful with regard to the meaning.[8]

Again, if He were above the universe, He would have a spatial relationship to it; and everything with a spatial relationship to a body must be either equal to it in size or smaller or larger than it, all of which would have to be measured out and appointed by another power. Far be it for the Unique Creator and Ruler to be subject to such a thing!

With regard to how one raises one's hands heavenwards when supplicating, this is [done] because heaven is the direction of supplication, and also because it symbolizes the majesty and exaltedness of the One to whom the supplication is directed; raising the hands upwards puts one in mind of His glory and highness. He تَعَالَىٰ is above every being in His power and might.[9]

THE EIGHTH FOUNDATION is knowledge that He تَعَالَىٰ is ascendant over His throne according to the sense He intends when He speaks of this ascendancy, which is neither inconsistent with His majesty nor related to the characteristics of contingency or temporality (*fanāʾ*). This is also what He means by ascendancy when He says in the Qurʾān, *Then He directed Himself to the heaven while it was smoke* [41:11]. This signifies nothing other than power and might,[10] as the poet said:

---

8 "However, in this case it should be asked, is the intention to declare His transcendence above that which does not befit His majesty? The one who uses the expression simply to designate Him with direction ought to be faulted for doing so, because this itself suggests something unbefitting [of God], and also because it does not accord with established lexical usage. If someone uses such language for any other intention, his words should also be rejected in order to safeguard against misguidance." Al-Zabīdī, *Itḥāf*, 2:104.

9 See al-Ghazālī's subtle explanation of the secret behind facing heaven for supplications in *al-Iqtiṣād*, 114, Eng. trans., 50–51. He chose the attributes of power and might becuase these are the attributes given special mention in the Book of God, *And He is the subjugator over His servants. And He is the Wise, the Acquainted* [*with all*] (6:18) and *the Most Merciful* [*who is*] *above the throne established* (20:5).

10 Al-Ghazālī says in *al-Iqtiṣād*, 126, Eng. trans., 59, "Therefore one of the predecessors"—it was Sufyān al-Thawrī—"said, 'I understand His words *the Most Merciful* [*who is*] *above the throne established* (20:5) in the same way as [I understand] His words *Then He directed Himself to the heaven while it was smoke* (41:11).

Bishr has ascended over Iraq,
Without drawing a sword or shedding blood.[11]

The people of truth are forced to make this interpretation just as the people of falsehood are forced to figuratively interpret God's words *He is with you wherever you are* [57:4], which all agree should be interpreted to symbolize [His being] All-Encompassing and All-Knowing. Likewise, [they agree that] the Prophet's صَلَّى ٱللَّهُ عَلَيْهِ وَسَلَّمَ words "The believer's heart is between two of the fingers of the All-Compassionate"[12] should be interpreted to symbolize omnipotence and power, and his words "The black stone is God's right hand on earth"[13] to symbolize honor and nobility. This is so because if they were to be taken literally, they would imply things that are impossible. Likewise, if ascendancy were to be taken literally as meaning "settling" or "sitting," it would imply that the one "sitting" is a body physically touching the throne, either the same size as it or larger or smaller than it. This is impossible, and everything that implies the impossible is itself impossible.

THE NINTH FOUNDATION is knowledge that, although He تَعَالَىٰ is transcendent above image and form, and exalted (*muqaddis*) above directions and locations, He will be seen with the eyes in the abode of the hereafter, the abode of perpetuity. The proof of this is that He تَعَالَىٰ says, [*Some*] *faces, that day, will be radiant, looking at their Lord* [75:22–23].[14] He cannot be seen in this world, [as is] verified by His saying, *Vision perceives Him not, but He perceives* [*all*] *vision* [6:103], and because He said to Moses عَلَيْهِ ٱلسَّلَامُ, *You will not see Me* [7:143].

Upon my word, how could the Muʿtazila know something about the attributes of the Lord of Lords that Moses عَلَيْهِ ٱلسَّلَامُ did not?[15]

---

11 The line was composed by al-Baʿīth al-Mujāshiʿī. See al-Thaʿālibī, *Yatīmat al-dahr*, 5:276, and al-Yāfaʿī, *Mirʾāt al-janān*, 1:148.

12 Muslim, 2654.

13 Al-Ḥākim al-Nīsābūrī, *al-Mustadrak*, 1:457; and al-Ṭabarānī, *al-Muʿjam al-awsaṭ*, 567, from ʿAbdallāh b. ʿAmr رَضِيَ ٱللَّهُ عَنْهُمَا.

14 "That is, immersed in the vision of His beauty to the extent that they will be oblivious of anything else." Al-Zabīdī, *Itḥāf*, 2:113.

15 His question implies that such is possible for God, for it is impossible that a prophet could be ignorant of what is possible and impossible for God while the Muʿtazila had knowledge of it. See *al-Iqtiṣād*, 138ff. Eng. trans., 70–72.

Or how could Moses عَلَيْهِ السَّلَامُ ask to see God when it is impossible? Ignorance befits foolish men of heresy and desires more than it does the prophets عَلَيْهِمُ السَّلَامُ!

As for the justification for taking the verse about the vision of God literally, it does not imply anything impossible, because vision is a kind of unveiling and knowledge, except that it is more complete and clearer than knowledge.[16] If it is possible to associate knowledge with Him although He is not in any direction, then it must be possible to associate vision with Him although He is not in any direction. Again, just as it is possible for God to see creation although He is not spatially related to it, it is possible for it to see Him without any spatial relationship. Again, just as it is possible for Him to be known without any modality or form, it is also possible for Him to be seen without any modality or form.

The tenth foundation is knowledge that God عَزَّوَجَلَّ is One without partner, and Unique without rival. He alone creates and originates, and He alone possesses the [ability to] bestow existence and origination. He has no peer to compete with Him or equal Him, nor any opposite to vie with Him or contest Him. The proof for this is found in His words *Had there been within the heavens and earth gods besides God, they both would have been ruined* [21:22].

This means that if there were two gods, and one of them willed something, the other would be either compelled to aid him, thereby showing himself to be subordinate and frail, thus not an all-powerful god, or else able to oppose and resist him, thereby having strength and power while showing the first to be weak and deficient, thus not an all-powerful god.

---

16 "If we look at the sun, for example, we see it and then our sight becomes blurred. We still know what the sun is when our sight is blurred, but in the moment before it blurs we know it even better. Likewise, when we know something perfectly well and then see it for the first time, we instinctively perceive (*nudrik bi-l-badīha*) the difference between the two states. This deeper perception is what we call vision." Ibn Abī l-Sharīf, *Kitāb al-Musāmara*, 1:37–38.

The Second Pillar of Faith: Knowledge of the Attributes of God

This pillar has ten foundations.

THE FIRST FOUNDATION is knowledge that the Creator of the world is Omnipotent, and that His words *And He is over all things powerful* [5:120] are true. The world is wisely ordained in its form and ordered in its innate character (*khilqa*); if a man sees a silken garment, beautifully designed and woven, symmetrically embroidered and proportioned, and tries to imagine its being woven by a dead person with no power or an incapacitated person, this would be contrary to his innate intelligence. Such could only be imagined by the foolish and the ignorant.

THE SECOND FOUNDATION is knowledge that He تَعَالَىٰ knows everything and encompasses all creation [with His knowledge]. Not a single atom on earth or in the heavens can evade His knowledge. He speaks the truth when He says, *He is Knowing of all things* [2:29], and guides to the truth of this with His words, *does He who created not know, while He is the Subtle, the Acquainted* [67:14].[17] With these words He guides you to take His creation as proof of His knowledge; for when you observe the significance of the subtleties and beautiful organization of creation, even in the smallest and weakest of things, you will not doubt in the Creator's knowledge of how to organize and construct it. The words of God سُبْحَانَهُ are the best form of guidance and explanation.

THE THIRD FOUNDATION is knowledge that God عَزَّوَجَلَّ is living. Anything confirmed to have knowledge and power must also have

17 Regarding the relevance of the name "the Subtle" or "the Gentle" (*al-Laṭīf*, from the noun *luṭf* meaning "subtlety" and "gentleness") to knowledge [of God], al-Ghazālī said, "This name can only rightly be given to one who knows the intricacies and depths of beneficial things, and all that is subtle in them, and then provides those who seek them with a path to them that is gentle, not violent. When gentleness of action and subtlety of perception are combined, that is what *luṭf* is. Perfection of this in knowledge and action can only belong to God عَزَّوَجَلَّ. His comprehensive knowledge of all subtle and hidden matters is not a separate category [of knowledge]; rather, His knowledge of hidden things is the same as His knowledge of open things, without any distinction between them." *Al-Maqṣad al-asnā*, 82, Eng. trans., 96–97.

life. If it were conceivable that a being have power, knowledge, action, and control, without being alive, it would be possible to doubt in the life of animals, even as they pass back and forth between motion and rest. Indeed, one could even doubt in the life of any craftsmen or producer. This would be to sink to the depths of ignorance and error.

THE FOURTH FOUNDATION is knowledge that He تَعَالَىٰ wills His action. Everything that exists depends on His will and proceeds forth from His desire. He is the one who originates things and brings them back, and He does what He wills. How could He not possess will, when for everything He does, He could have done the opposite? Even for those things that do not have an opposite, He could have done them earlier or later than He did, for [having] power [over the] single event means [having power over its] opposites and the timing [of the event].

Therefore there must be a will that directs the power into doing one or the other. Moreover, if knowledge did not require a will to specify the known thing, such that it could be said that it merely came into existence at a time prior to which there was knowledge of its existence, then it would be permissible that [knowledge] did not require power, such that it could be said that it came into existence without power because the knowledge of its existence preceded it.[18]

THE FIFTH FOUNDATION is knowledge that He تَعَالَىٰ is hearing and seeing. The concepts of the mind and the secrets of imagination and thought do not evade His sight, and the sound of a black ant creeping across a great rock on a dark night does not elude His hearing. How could He not be hearing and seeing when hearing and sight are undoubtedly perfections and not deficiencies? How could a creature be more perfect than the creator, or the product more noble and complete than the maker? How could the apportionment be equitable when the deficiency occurs on His part and the perfection on His creation and product?

Consider also the argument of Abraham عَلَيْهِ السَّلَامُ against his father, who worshiped idols in ignorance and delusion. He said to him, *why do you worship that which does not hear and does not see and will not benefit you at all?* [19:42]. If this argument could

18 Al-Ghazālī explained the rebuttal to this in *al-Iqtiṣād*, 169, Eng. trans., 105ff., as did al-Juwaynī in *al-Irshād*, 64.

be turned on him with respect to his own object of worship, his argument would be invalid and his evidence would be worthless. It would disprove God's own words: *And that was Our* [*conclusive*] *argument which We gave Abraham against his people* [6:83]. Just as it is conceivable that He acts without limbs and knows without a heart or brain, so too it is conceivable that He sees without eyes and hears without ears, for there is no difference.

THE SIXTH FOUNDATION is that He تَعَالَىٰ is a speaker with speech that is an attribute existing in His essence without a voice or letters. His speech no more resembles the speech of anyone else than His being resembles the being of anyone else. In reality, speech is the speech of the soul; vocal speech composed of letters serves only to express this speech, just as it can also be expressed sometimes through gestures and motions. How could this have escaped the attention of certain weak-minded people, when even the ignorant pre-Islamic poets knew about it, one of them having said:[19]

> Speech is in the heart, and it is merely
> The tongue making the heart evident.

There may be a person whose intellect does not serve him and whose mind does not restrain him from saying, "My tongue is contingent, but what is uttered by it with my contingent power is eternal (*qadīm*)." Spare yourself from engaging with such a mind, and restrain your tongue from addressing him. Someone may not understand that "eternal" means that which is not preceded by anything, and that the letter "B" comes before the letter "S" in your statement "***Bismillāh***," and that therefore the "S" following the "B" is not an eternal [statement]. Thus free your heart from any regard for him. God سُبۡحَانَهُ possesses the secret concerning distancing some of His creatures; *and whomever God leaves astray—there will be for him no guide* [13:33].

Again, someone might find it far-fetched that in this world, Moses عَلَيۡهِ ٱلسَّلَامُ heard speech that was not composed of a voice or letters. Let him then also deny that in the hereafter, a being will be

19 This line has been attributed to al-Akhṭal, though it is not in his *Dīwān*, and also to Ibn Ṣamṣām al-Raqāsh, *Dhayl mirʾāt al-zamān*, 3:189, as cited in al-Zabīdī, *Itḥāf*, 2:146.

seen who has neither body nor color. If he can conceive of seeing a being with no body, color, form, or quantity, though now he cannot see any other kind of being, let him conceive for the sense of hearing what he can already conceive for the sense of sight. If he can conceive that God has a knowledge that encompasses all beings, let him conceive that His essence has an attribute of speech which encompasses all that could be expressed in words.

If he can conceive that the nature of the seven heavens and the nature of paradise and hell are written on a small page and preserved in a minute portion of the heart, and that all of this can be seen with the tiny pupil of the eye without thereby the heavens, earth, paradise, and hell being contained inside that pupil, heart, or page, then let him conceive of the nature of speech recited by tongues, preserved in hearts, and written in copies of the Qurʾān, without the incarnation of that speech being in them. If speech itself were located in the book wherein it is written, then God's essence would be located on the page whereon His name is written, and the essence of fire would be located on the page whereon its name is written, and the page would burst into flames.

The seventh foundation is that His speech, which exists in His essence, is eternal (*qadīm*), as are all of His attributes. It is impossible that [the speech] could be subject to contingencies and affected by change. On the contrary, [God's] attributes must necessarily be eternal (*qadam*) just as [God's] essence is neither subject to change nor a locus for contingencies. In His beginninglessness and eternal endlessness, He is, was and ever will be endowed with His glorious attributes and free from any change. If something is subject to contingencies, it can never be independent of them; and something that cannot be independent of contingencies must itself be contingent. The only thing that proves the contingent nature of bodies is that they are subject to change and shifting attributes. How, then, could their Creator share their propensity to change? All of this proves that His speech exists eternally in His essence, and that the voices that express it are the only contingent things.

It is perfectly conceivable that a father could hope and desire that his unborn child should seek an education, and that after his child is born and reaches maturity God might create in him knowledge of his father's desire, so that he becomes bound to follow the desire that remained secret in his father's heart until the child came to know of it. Likewise, it is equally conceivable that the desire expressed in God's command to Moses عَلَيْهِ ٱلسَّلَامُ, *Remove your sandals* [20:12], could have remained secret in the essence of God عَزَّوَجَلَّ, and that it was the fate of Moses to be addressed with these words after he came into being, once knowledge of this command had been created in him and he heard that beginningless speech.[20]

The eighth foundation is that His knowledge is eternal (*qadīm*). He has never ceased knowing in His essence and attributes. Whatever His creatures do, and whenever His creatures do something, that knowledge does not occur to Him newly, but rather it exists, fully disclosed to Him through His eternal (*azalī*) knowledge. Imagine that we were provided knowledge that Zayd would arrive at sunrise, and that this knowledge remained accurate until sunrise. Zayd's arrival at sunrise would be known to us by means of this knowledge, without the need for any new knowledge. This is how the eternality (*qadam*) of God's knowledge should be understood.

The ninth foundation is that His will is eternal. It is eternally attached to the engendering of all contingent things at their appropriate times in accordance with the priority of knowledge without beginning (*al-ʿilm al-azalī*). If [His will] were itself contingent, then He would be a locus for contingencies. If it occurred extraneous to His essence, then He would not be the one willing it, just as you cannot move with a motion that is outside yourself. No matter how you attempt to imagine this, the will would always need another will to bring it into being, and that other will would itself need another to bring it into being, and so on ad infinitum. Were it possible for a will to come into existence without being willed [by another being], then it would be equally possible for the world to come into existence without being willed [by another being].

---

20 The verb "to hear" (*samiʿ*) is made transitive by use of the preposition "to" (*li*) as it is used here and in the example "God listens to whoever praises Him." Al-Zabīdī, *Itḥāf*, 2:152. Furthermore, "listening to something" is associated with cognition. However, if someone makes his listening to the Qurʾān the same as listening to the actual eternal speech [of God], he has negated the excellent quality that is specified for our master Moses عَلَيْهِ ٱلسَّلَامُ.

THE TENTH FOUNDATION is that God تَعَالَىٰ is Knowing with knowledge, Living with life, Omnipotent with omnipotence, Volitional with will, Speaking with speech, Hearing with hearing, and Seeing with sight.[21] He has these qualities that stem from His eternal attributes. To say "knowing without knowledge" is just like saying "rich without wealth," "knowledge without a knower" or "a knower without anything known." Knowledge, the known, and the knower are as inseparable as killing, the killed, and the killer. Just as it is inconceivable that there be a killer without a killing and a killed, or a killed without a killer and a killing, it is equally inconceivable to imagine a knower without knowledge, knowledge without a known, or a known without a knower. These three are inseparable in the mind, and cannot be detached from one another. Anyone who deems it possible for the knower to be detached from knowledge must necessarily deem it equally possible for it to be detached from the known, or knowledge detached from the knower, because there is no difference between these qualities.[22]

21 "The theologians are divided into two [groups]: those who affirm the theory of 'modes' (*aḥwāl*), and those who deny it. Those who affirm it, such as the *qāḍī*, the *imām*, and the author [al-Ghazālī] use the expression 'Knowing with knowledge, Living with life…', while those who deny it use the expression 'Knowing and has knowledge, Living and has life.'" Al-Zabīdī, *Itḥāf*, 2:153.

22 "The reason we affirm these attributes as well as the understanding of the essence is that He تَعَالَىٰ used these names to refer to Himself in His book on the tongue of His Prophet, addressing the native speakers of this language; and in that language, a 'knower' means a being with knowledge, 'powerful' means a being with power…" Al-Zabīdī, *Itḥāf*, 2:154.

The Third Pillar of Faith: Knowledge of the Acts of God

This pillar has ten foundations.

THE FIRST FOUNDATION is knowledge that every contingent thing in the universe is His act, His creation, and His design.[23] They were created by none other than Him, and given being by none other than Him. He created humankind and their deeds, and gave being to their power and motion. All the actions of His creatures are created by Him and dependent on His power, as is confirmed in His تَعَالَىٰ words, *God is the Creator of all things* [39:62]; *While God created you and what you do* [37:96]; and again, *And conceal your speech or publicize it; indeed, He is Knowing of that within the breasts. Does He who created not know, while He is the Subtle, the Acquainted* [67:13–14].

He commanded His servants to be cautious in their words, deeds, secrets, and thoughts, because He knows the sources of their actions. This infers knowledge about creation. How could He not be the Creator of His servant's actions, when His omnipotence is complete and without deficiency, and governs the motions of His servants' bodies? The movements are homogeneous in nature, and His omnipotence governs them all intrinsically. What would keep it from governing some of them and not others, when they are homogeneous in nature? How could animals monopolize design? The spider, the bee, and all the animals produce such subtleties of design as to make intelligent men marvel; how could they achieve such design alone without the aid of the Lord of Lords, when they do not even know the details of what they do? Far be it! These creatures are weak and lowly, and all sovereignty and dominion belong to the Compeller (*al-Jabbār*) of earth and heaven.

---

23 "The attributes are of two kinds: attributes of essence and attributes of act. The difference between them is that any attribute of God تَعَالَىٰ whose opposite cannot be His attribute is an attribute of essence; these include omnipotence, knowledge, might, and glory. Then any attribute of God whose opposite can also be His attribute is an attribute of act; these include clemency, mercy, condemnation, and anger." Al-Zabīdī, *Itḥāf*, 2:157.

THE SECOND FOUNDATION: Although God تَعَالَىٰ is the sole creator of humankind's deeds, they are still under each person's power by means of acquisition. God تَعَالَىٰ creates both the power and the deed, and creates the choice (*ikhtiyār*) and the chosen (*mukhtār*). The power is a quality of the servant and a creation of the Lord سُبْحَانَهُ, not acquired by Him. The deed is a creation of the Lord تَعَالَىٰ and a quality of the servant, being acquired by him. It has been created as the object of a power, which is a quality of his; the deed has a relation to another attribute called "power," and with respect to this relationship it is called "acquisition."

How could it be absolute compulsion, when [every man] necessarily grasps the difference between a predestined action and an involuntary shiver? And conversely, how could it be created by the servant when he does not have comprehensive knowledge of the details of all aspects of his acquired deed, nor their number?[24]

Since both extremes have been shown to be false, there remains only the way of moderation in creed, namely that deeds are the object of God's power as creation, and the object of a person's power in another kind of relationship which is called acquisition.[25] It is not necessary that the connection of power to its object be through creation alone, since God's power was connected to the world from all eternity, even before the world was created; and then when creation occurred, it was connected to it in another way. This shows that the relationship of power is not limited to the actual creation of its object.

THE THIRD FOUNDATION: Although the servant's deed is acquired by him, this does not mean it is not willed by God تَعَالَىٰ. Nothing happens in the worldly kingdom or the realm of spiritual domain, not even the blink of an eye, a fleeting thought, or a passing glance, except by God's ordainment (*qaḍāʾ*) and determination (*qadar*), and by His desire (*irāda*) and will (*mashīʾa*). From Him are good and

---

24 These rhetorical questions are meant as a rebuttal of the Jabariyya and Muʿtazila sects and to lay the foundation for the Sunnī position.

25 This is based on the literal import of the verse, *it* [*the soul*] *will have* [*the consequence of*] *what* [*good*] *it has gained, and it will bear* [*the consequence of*] *what* [*evil*] *it has earned* (2:286). The Māturīdī school calls it "choice" (*ikhtiyār*), this term being more suggestive of the human being's power to choose.

evil, benefit and harm, Islam and disbelief, recognition and denial, victory and defeat, error and guidance, obedience and disobedience, idolatry and faith. Nothing can rebuff His ordainment, nor amend His judgment. God sends astray [thereby] whom He wills and guides whom He wills.[26] *He is not questioned about what He does, but they will be questioned* [21:23].[27]

Transmitted reports indicate this, such as the unanimous statement of the Muslim community that "What God wills comes to pass, and what He does not will does not,"[28] as well as God's عَزَّوَجَلَّ words *had God willed, He would have guided the people* [13:31], and *if We had willed, We could have given every soul its guidance* [32:13].

Rational proofs also indicate this, such as the observation that if God hated sins and crimes and did not desire them, and if they were naught but the will of the Devil (*iblīs*), may God curse him, who is an enemy of God سُبۡحَانَهُ, this would mean that the enemy's will would be more successful than the will of God Himself تَعَالَىٰ.

Upon my word, could any Muslim permit himself to reduce the sovereignty of the All-Compelling (*al-Jabbār*), the Sublime and Generous, to a level that even a village leader would not accept for himself? If the leader's enemy had more control over the village than the leader did, he would disdain his own leadership and resign his position. Now disobedience is the prevalent state for humankind, and according to the heretics this all takes place against the will of the Truth تَعَالَىٰ (*al-Ḥaqq*), which would reduce Him to the depths of weakness and incapacity—and the Lord of Lords, Most-Lofty and Great, is ever exalted above the claims of the unjust! In any case, the more apparent it becomes that the deeds of humankind are created by God تَعَالَىٰ, the more clearly it is established that they are also willed by Him.

---

26 This is a paraphrase of Qurʾān 14:4.

27 We consider "certain beings 'evil' based on their relation to us and the harm they pose us, not on what they are when they come from God. Thus the creation of evil is not an ugly act; nothing God does is evil." Al-Zabīdī, *Itḥāf*, 2:172.

28 This is part of a *ḥadīth* in Abū Dāwūd, 5075, part of a statement taught by the Messenger of God صَلَّىٰٱللَّهُعَلَيۡهِوَسَلَّمَ to one of his daughters. It is cited here to refute the Muʿtazila claim that there are created things, such as disbelief and sin, that God dislikes and does not desire.

Here someone might ask, "Why, then, does He forbid what He wills and command what He wills not?" Our answer is that command is not the same thing as will. Consider [this]: A man beats his slave, and the sultan rebukes him for this. He argues that his action was justified because the slave disobeyed him, but the sultan does not believe him. The man seeks to prove his case by giving a command to his slave which he knows the slave will disobey before the sultan's eyes. So he says to him, in the sultan's presence, "Saddle this beast." Thus he issues him a command that he does not want to see obeyed. If he did not issue the command, then the excuse he proffered to the sultan would not be proven; and if he actually wanted the command to be obeyed, this would amount to seeking his own ruin, which is absurd.

THE FOURTH FOUNDATION: God تَعَالَى is gracious in creating and originating, and bestows favor by placing responsibility on the servants, and there is no obligation on Him to create and place responsiblity. The Muʿtazila[29] say that He is obliged to do this for the good of the servants. This is impossible because He is the one who obligates, commands, and prohibits; how could He be liable to any obligation or subject to any compulsion or order?

The concept of an "obligation" has two meanings. The first describes an action that must be done in order to avoid harm, whether in the long run, as in saying, "A servant must obey God, or He will punish him with hell in the hereafter," or in the short run, as in saying, "A thirsty man must drink water or he will die." The second meaning refers to something, the non-existence of which conveys an impossibility, such as saying that an object of knowledge is obligatory because its non-existence conveys an impossibility, namely that knowledge would become ignorance.

Now if our opponent means that creation is obligatory for God according to the first sense, he thereby implies that He is subject to harm. If he means it according to the second sense, then this can be allowed because once knowledge is established to exist, the object

29 In *al-Iqtiṣād*, 233, Eng. trans., 170, al-Ghazālī ascribes this position to "some of the Muʿtazila"; the Muʿtazila of Basra did not adhere to this belief.

of knowledge must also exist.[30] If he means a third sense aside from these two, he has not made himself intelligible.

As for his claim that God is obliged to do this "for the good of His servants," it is simply false. God would not be harmed by refraining from doing what is most beneficial for His servants, and thus this obligation would be meaningless. Besides, it would be more beneficial for the servants for Him to create them in paradise, rather than creating them in a world filled with tribulations and giving them the ability to sin, thereby exposing them to the dangers of punishment and the terrors of resurrection and reckoning. An intelligent person could hardly call that a state of bliss.

The fifth foundation: Contrary to the Muʿtazila, it is possible for God سُبْحَانَهُ to charge His servants with more than they could bear. If He were not able to do this, it would be absurd to ask Him not to, yet they did ask Him this: *Our Lord, and burden us not with that which we have no ability to bear* [2:286].

Moreover, God تَعَالَىٰ told His Prophet صَلَّىٰ ٱللَّٰهُ عَلَيْهِ وَسَلَّمَ that Abū Jahl would not believe in him. Then He commanded [Abū Jahl] to believe in all that He said. And one of the things He said was "that [Abū Jahl] does not believe in [God]," so how could [Abū Jahl] believe in [God] given that [God] said he would never believe in Him? Is that anything other than impossible?

The sixth foundation: Contrary to the Muʿtazila, God عَزَّ وَجَلَّ has the power to torment and punish people without their being guilty of any crime in the past, nor with any promised reward in the future. He can do as He wills with what belongs to Him, and it is inconceivable that His control goes beyond what is not in His possession.[31] Injustice means to dispose of what belongs to another without his permission, and this is impossible for God تَعَالَىٰ because no one else possesses anything of which He could unjustly dispose.

The proof that this is possible is that it actually occurs: slaughtering animals causes them pain, and human beings deal them all manner of torments though they are guilty of no crime. One might

30 That is, it would be correct to say, "God must have created the universe" in the sense of "given that the universe exists, God must have been the one to create it."

31 That is, His control is limited to His possessions (and everything He created is in His possession).

say, "God will resurrect them and reward them for the pains they suffered, and God سُبْحَانَهُ is obliged to do so."

Our response to this is that if someone believes that God is obliged to resurrect every ant trodden upon and every insect crushed so that He can reward them for their pains, such a person has strayed from the law and from reason. If he means that God is obliged to resurrect and reward them because He would be harmed if He did not, then this is impossible; and if he means something else, we have already seen that this would be incomprehensible because it would stray from the aforementioned meanings of the word "obligation."[32]

THE SEVENTH FOUNDATION: God تَعَالَىٰ does what He wills with His servants. He is not obliged to do what is most beneficial for His servants because of what we have said about nothing being obligatory for Him; indeed, it is not even rationally conceivable that He could be obliged to do anything. *He is not questioned about what He does, but they will be questioned* [21:23].

Upon my word, how could the Muʿtazila, who hold that God is obliged always to do what is most beneficial, respond to this issue that we put forth to him: Suppose that in the hereafter there is a child and an adult who both died as Muslims. According to the Muʿtazila, God is obliged to raise the level of the adult and prefer him to the boy because of how he toiled with faith and obedience after reaching adulthood. Were the child to say, "O my Lord, why did you raise his rank over mine?" He would say, "He reached adulthood and toiled with acts of obedience." The child would say, "You caused me to die in my childhood, but You should have kept me alive so that I could reach adulthood and toil. You swerved

---

32 This is explained in *al-Iqtiṣād*, 222, Eng. trans., 158 and 241–242, Eng. trans., 177–178. Al-Zabīdī said, "As for what Aḥmad [b. Ḥanbal] narrated with an authentic chain, 'Creatures will receive their rights from one another, even the hornless ram from the horned ram, and even an atom from an atom.'" This was also narrated by Muslim, 2582, with the wording "All beings will be given their rights on the day of resurrection, even the hornless ram from the horned ram." "What this means is that God will either visit upon them the pain that He knows they dealt out, or that He will literally allow the victims to exact their own retribution. This is not rationally impossible in our view, but we do not say it will necessarily be so; that is, we do not say that God is obliged to do it, as the Muʿtazila say. This is better than simply dismissing it as being from the reports of lone narrators and therefore not certain, certitude being required for matters of creed." Al-Zabīdī, *Itḥāf*, 2:185.

from justice to favor him with a longer life than me. Why did you favor him so?" God تَعَالَىٰ would answer, "Because I knew that if you had reached adulthood, you would have fallen into idolatry or sin, and therefore it was better for you to die in childhood." This is the excuse that the Muʿtazila would offer on behalf of God عَزَّوَجَلَّ. But then the disbelievers would cry out from the depths of hell, "O our Lord, did you not know that when we reached adulthood we would fall into idolatry? You ought to have caused us to die in childhood, and we would have been happy with a rank even lower than that of the Muslim child." What possible response could there be to this? Is there anything left to do but acknowledge that matters [of God] are too gloriously exalted to be judged by the logic of the Muʿtazila.

Here someone might say, "If He is able to do what is most beneficial for His servants, but then subjects them to what causes punishment, this is ugly and contrary to wisdom." Our response is that the meaning of "ugly" (*qabīḥ*) is that which does not accord with one's yearning (*gharaḍ*). Something can be ugly to one person and pleasing to another if it accords with the latter's yearning but not the former's. A person's murder is ugly to his allies and pleasing to his enemies. So if what is meant by "ugly" is that which does not accord with the Creator's سُبْحَانَهُ yearning, then this is impossible because He has no yearning, and thus it is inconceivable that anything ugly could come from Him. Likewise, it is inconceivable that He could be unjust because it is inconceivable that He could dispose of what belongs to others. If, on the other hand, by "ugly" is meant that which does not accord with someone else's yearning, then why would you say that this is impossible for Him? Is this anything but a baseless desire that is contrary to that which is attested to by the complaint of the people of hell we described earlier?

Moreover, the meaning of "wise" (*ḥakīm*) is one who knows the reality of things and is able to do them perfectly according to his will. Why should this create an obligation to seek what is most beneficial (for others)? A wise man seeks what is most beneficial for himself so that he can earn regard in this world and reward in the next, or ward off harm from himself. All this is impossible for God سُبْحَانَهُ.

The eighth foundation: Recognition of God سُبْحَانَهُ and [knowledge that]obedience to Him are obligations imposed by God تَعَالَىٰ and His law, and not by reason. This is in contrast to the Muʿtazila because if reason dictated obedience, it would either not be beneficial, which is impossible because reason cannot dictate something pointless, or be beneficial and desirable. In this case, [the benefit] must either refer to the object of worship, which is impossible in relation to Him تَعَالَىٰ because His holiness frees Him from desires and benefits and moreover, faith, disbelief, obedience, and rebellion are alike to Him, or it must refer to the desires of the worshiper, which is also impossible because he has no desires [for obedience] in the present sense. Rather, he must toil for it and deny himself desires because of it, and in the future sense, there is only reward or punishment. But how could he know that God تَعَالَىٰ rewards recognition and obedience and does not punish that, since for him obedience and rebellion are alike, and he has no inclination toward, or identification with either of them? This distinction can only be known through the law.

It is a mistake to draw an analogy in this regard between the Creator and the creature because creatures distinguish between gratitude and ingratitude based on how they are pleased, excited, and gratified by one and not the other.

Here someone might say, "If consideration and realization are made obligatory only by the law, and the law cannot be established for a morally responsible person unless he first considers it, then such a person could say to a prophet, 'Reason does not compel me to consideration, and the law cannot be confirmed for me unless I consider it, so I cannot proceed with the consideration.' The messenger would have no answer for this."

Our response is this: Imagine that someone were to say to a man standing in a certain place, "There is a fierce lion behind you, and if you do not move, it will kill you. If you look behind you, you will see it and know that I am telling the truth." The man says, "As long as I do not look behind me, it will not be established that you are telling the truth, and I will not look behind me as long as it is not established that you are telling the truth." All this will prove is the man's idiocy and self-destructive tendency; it will not harm the warner at all.

Likewise, the Prophet ﷺ said, "Death is behind you, and fierce lions and burning flames lie in wait beyond it unless you guard yourself from them. You can recognize that I am telling the truth by observing my miracle. Those who observe it will recognize it, guard themselves, and be saved; those who do not observe it and persist in their stubbornness will come to ruin and perdition. It would not harm me if all people went to ruin, for my sole obligation is to deliver the message."

The law tells us that there will be fierce lions in the hereafter, and reason allows us to understand what it says and comprehend the possibility of what it says about the future. Human nature encourages us to guard ourselves against harm. An obligation is something that it is harmful to neglect, and the role of the law as a giver of obligations is to tell us about potential harms. Reason then tells us that we should not expose ourselves to harm in the hereafter by indulging our lusts.

This is the meaning of the law and reason and how they participate in defining obligations. Were it not for the fear of punishment for neglecting what the law commands, no obligation would be confirmed because the concept of obligation is meaningless unless it relates to a harm in the hereafter resulting from neglect of it.

THE NINTH FOUNDATION: The sending of the prophets عَلَيْهِمُ السَّلَامُ is not impossible, contrary to the Brahmans,[33] who said that there would be no benefit in sending prophets because reason can fulfill their role. [This is false] because reason cannot guide one to the acts that lead to salvation in the hereafter any more than it can guide one to the medicines that bring health. People need prophets just as they need doctors.[34] However, the veracity of a doctor is ascertained through experience, while the veracity of a prophet is ascertained through miracles.

---

33 The Arabic term is *al-barāhima*. The term is used in a broad sense to refer to Indian philosophers associated with the Upanishads. There is a trend of thought in Indian philosophy that rejects prophecy based on the sufficiency of the human intellect. See Nasr and Leaman (eds.), *History of Islamic Philosophy,* 1:54–55, 1:64–65.

34 "Because the role of the messenger is to be the ambassador of the Real to His servants, to cure those ailments of theirs that their minds cannot identify." Al-Zabīdī, *Itḥāf,* 2:198.

THE TENTH FOUNDATION: God سُبْحَانَهُ sent Muḥammad صَلَّى ٱللَّٰهُ عَلَيْهِ وَسَلَّمَ to be the seal of the prophets and to abrogate the laws of the Jews, Christians, and Sabians that preceded him. He aided him with plain miracles and clear signs such as the splitting of the moon,[35] the glorification of the pebbles [in his hand],[36] the causing of the mute to speak,[37] and the water that flowed from between his fingers.[38]

Another of his clear signs, with which he challenged all the Arabs, was the glorious Qurʾān. Despite their distinction in eloquence and rhetoric, and their attempts to defame him, silence him, kill him, and banish him, as God عَزَّوَجَلَّ tells us, they were not able to confront him with anything like the Qurʾān. This is [true] because it is beyond human power to imitate the combined eloquence and arrangement of the Qurʾān, much less the reports about the previous generations it contains, though the Prophet was unlettered and unfamiliar with books and their predictions about unseen matters that were later revealed to be accurate. These include His words, *You will surely enter al-Masjid al-Ḥarām, if God wills, in safety, with your heads shaved and [hair] shortened* [48:27], and His words, *Alif Lām Mīm. The Byzantines have been defeated in the nearest land but they, after their defeat, will overcome within a few years* [30:1–4].

A miracle is valuable in proving the veracity of a messenger because if something is beyond man's power, it must be an act of God تَعَالَىٰ. Therefore when a miracle accompanies the claim of a prophet, this amounts to God's confirmation of his veracity. This is like the example of a man [who] stands before a king and announces to [the king's] subjects that he is the king's envoy to them. If he says to the king, "If I am truthful, then stand up and sit down on your throne three times in a manner contrary to your normal habit," and the king does this, the people present will know for certain that the king has confirmed the veracity of his envoy.

35 Al-Bukhārī, 3637; and Muslim, 4109.

36 Al-Ṭabarānī, *al-Muʿjam al-awsaṭ*, 4109.

37 Abū Dāwūd, 2675.

38 Al-Bukhārī, 3572; and Muslim, 2279.

The Fourth Pillar of Faith: Belief Based on Transmitted Reports and Believing in What [the Prophet ﷺ] Conveyed about God

This pillar has ten foundations.

THE FIRST FOUNDATION is the gathering and reckoning. The law attests to this, and it is real, and it is obligatory to believe in it because it is rationally possible. It means that there is a resurrection after annihilation, which is just as possible for God to do as it was to create [people] in the first place, as *He says, "Who will give life to bones, while they are distintegrated?" Say, "He will give them life who produced them the first time"* [36:78–79]. Thus He cited the first creation as proof of the resurrection. He عَزَّوَجَلَّ also says, *Your creation and your resurrection will not be but as that of a single soul* [31:28].

THE SECOND FOUNDATION is the questioning of Munkar and Nakīr. This is attested to by reports, and believing in it is obligatory because it is possible and requires nothing more than the return of life to that part of the body that can understand speech. This is intrinsically possible, and is not disproven by the observed stillness of the dead body or the fact that we cannot hear the questions posed to it. A sleeping person appears to be motionless, yet he inwardly feels pain and pleasure and notices their effects when he wakens. The Messenger of God صَلَّى ٱللَّهُ عَلَيْهِ وَسَلَّمَ could hear the words of Gabriel عَلَيْهِ ٱلسَّلَامُ and see him, while those around him could neither see nor hear him.[39] *They encompass not a thing of His knowledge except for what He wills* [2:255], and unless He creates hearing and sight in them, they cannot perceive anything.

THE THIRD FOUNDATION is the punishment of the grave,[40] to which the law attests. God says, *the fire, they are exposed to it morning and evening. And the day the hour appears* [*it will be said*], *"Make*

39 Al-Bukhārī, 3217; and Muslim, 2447.

40 "This is the punishment [that takes place during] the isthmus (*barzakh*), [it is] named the [punishment of the] grave because this is the usual place for it. Any dead person whom God wishes to punish will be punished regardless of whether or not he is buried in a grave. All agree that it is visited upon both the spirit and the body." Al-Zabīdī, *Itḥāf*, 2:37.

the people of Pharaoh enter the severest punishment" [40:46].[41] Both the Messenger of God ﷺ and the righteous predecessors were known to pray for refuge from the punishment of the grave.[42] It is also possible, and therefore it is obligatory to believe in it. The fact that a dead body can be divided in the bellies of lions and the gizzards of birds is no reason not to believe in it, because living beings sense pain through specific parts of the body, to which God تَعَالَىٰ is well able to restore sensation.

The fourth foundation: The balance (*mīzān*) is real.[43] God تَعَالَىٰ says, *We place the scales of justice for the Day of Resurrection* [21:47], and, *So those whose scales are heavy—it is they who will be the successful. And those whose scales are light—they are the ones who will lose themselves* [7:8–9]. This means that God تَعَالَىٰ will assign a weight to the written records of deeds according to the levels of those deeds in His reckoning. This will make the value of humankind's deeds visible to them, so that they can see the justice of their punishment, or the grace of their forgiveness and manifold reward.

The fifth foundation: The traverse (*ṣirāṭ*) spans over the plain of hell. It is finer than a hair and narrower than a sword's blade.[44] God تَعَالَىٰ says, *guide them to the path of hellfire and stop them; indeed, they are to be questioned* [37:23–24]. This is possible, and therefore it is obligatory to believe in it; for He who has the power to make birds fly in the air has the power to make a person pass over the traverse.[45]

The sixth foundation: paradise and hell have already been created. God تَعَالَىٰ says, *and hasten to forgiveness from your Lord and a garden as wide as the heavens and earth, prepared for the righteous* [3:133]. His word *prepared* indicates that it has already been created, and since this is not impossible it should be taken literally. There are no grounds for objecting that it is useless to create them before

---

41 "God also says about the people of Noah عَلَيْهِ السَّلَامُ, *Because of their sins they were drowned and put into the fire* (71:25); that is, instantly, without delay, as indicated by the preposition *fa*." Al-Zabīdī, *Itḥāf*, 2:218.

42 Muslim, 2867.

43 Therefore we are not permitted to interpret it, as the Muʿtazila did, as a metaphor for justice.

44 Muslim, 183, as a saying of Abū Saʿīd al-Khudrī.

45 Al-Ghazālī mentioned the pool (*al-ḥawḍ*) in chapter 1.

the day of reckoning, because God تَعَالَىٰ *is not questioned about what He does, but they will be questioned* [21:23].

The seventh foundation: The true *imām* after the Messenger of God صَلَّىٰ ٱللَّٰهُ عَلَيْهِ وَسَلَّمَ was Abū Bakr, then ʿUmar, then ʿUthmān, then ʿAlī رَضِيَ ٱللَّٰهُ عَنْهُمْ. The Messenger of God صَلَّىٰ ٱللَّٰهُ عَلَيْهِ وَسَلَّمَ did not appoint any *imām* himself; if he had done so, the appointment would certainly have been better known than the appointments he made of governors and military leaders throughout the land. Those appointments were no secret, so how could the appointment of [an *imām*] have been secret? And if it was made openly, then how could it subsequently have vanished from memory and not been transmitted to us? Thus Abū Bakr was appointed *imām* solely by being elected and having allegiance pledged to him. As for the suggestion that [the Prophet] did appoint someone else rather than him, this amounts to accusing all the Companions of disobeying the Messenger of God صَلَّىٰ ٱللَّٰهُ عَلَيْهِ وَسَلَّمَ, as well as violating the consensus [*ijmāʿ* of the community]. None would dare to suggest such a thing but the Rawāfiḍ.[46]

For the people of the *sunna*, it is part of faith to uphold the integrity of all the Companions, and to praise them just as God سُبْحَانَهُ and His Messenger صَلَّىٰ ٱللَّٰهُ عَلَيْهِ وَسَلَّمَ praised them. The dispute between Muʿāwiya and ʿAlī رَضِيَ ٱللَّٰهُ عَنْهُمْ arose from a difference of honest and informed opinion, not an attempt on Muʿāwiya's part to seize the *imāma* [caliphate]. ʿAlī's رَضِيَ ٱللَّٰهُ عَنْهُ view was that handing over the killers of ʿUthmān رَضِيَ ٱللَّٰهُ عَنْهُ would cause turmoil in the early days of his *imāma* [caliphate] because of their many tribal and military connections, and therefore he deemed that it was better to delay it. Muʿāwiya رَضِيَ ٱللَّٰهُ عَنْهُ, on the other hand, deemed that delaying their fate, given the severity of their crime, would encourage further attacks on *imāms* and would result in bloodshed. Among the virtuous scholars, some have said that everyone who offers an honest and informed opinion is correct, while others have said that only one

---

46 "They are called *rāfiḍa* [rejecters] because they left Zayd b. ʿAlī رَضِيَ ٱللَّٰهُ عَنْهُ when he forbade them from vilifying the Companions; when they learned what he had said and that he refused to renounce the *shaykhayn* [Abū Bakr and ʿUmar رَضِيَ ٱللَّٰهُ عَنْهُمَا], they rejected him." Al-Zabīdī, *Itḥāf*, 2:223.

side of a dispute can be correct. Yet no man of learning ever said that ʿAlī رَضِيَ ٱللَّهُ عَنْهُ was wrong.[47]

THE EIGHTH FOUNDATION: The virtues of the Companions رَضِيَ ٱللَّهُ عَنْهُمْ is according to the order of their succession to the caliphate. True virue is that which is virtuous in the sight of God تَعَالَىٰ, and none but the Messenger of God صَلَّى ٱللَّهُ عَلَيْهِ وَسَلَّمَ can know this. There are many verses and reports praising them all,[48] and only those who were present at the time of revelation and witness to its contextual circumstances and details could be cognizant of the nature of this virtue and its hierarchy. Had they not understood this, they would not have ordered the affair in the way they did; for they could not be swayed from the path of God by the reproach of any reproacher,[49] nor deviated from the truth by any deviator.

THE NINTH FOUNDATION: The conditions of suitability for the *imāma*, after Islam and soundness of mind, are five: masculinity,

---

47 Moreover, the mainstream view is that [ʿAlī] رَضِيَ ٱللَّهُ عَنْهُ was correct in his reasoning. Al-Zabīdī quotes al-Shihāb al-Dīn al-Suhrawardī's treatise *Aʿlām al-hudā wa-ʿaqīdat arbāb al-tuqā* as follows: "O you who would be free of passion and factionalism, know that although the Companions رَضِيَ ٱللَّهُ عَنْهُمْ had pure hearts, they were nevertheless human beings possessed of human egos (*nufūs*); and egos have attributes which will sometimes surface. When an attribute of their egos surfaced that their hearts rejected, they would follow the verdict of their hearts and reject what arose from their egos. Yet small remnants of what arose from their egos would then be transferred to other people who were all ego and no heart, and had no perception of the heart's judgment. Such people would instinctively follow their egotistical identities (*al-jinsiyya al-nafsiyya*), and base their actions on the outward implications of this, and thus they fell into heresies, doubts, and temptations, and drank every poisoned drink. If you wish for advice, then here it is: refrain from delving into their affair, and love all of them equally, and leave aside the details." Al-Zabīdī, *Itḥāf*, 2:229.

48 Al-Bukhārī, 3673; and Muslim, 2540, the Prophet صَلَّى ٱللَّهُ عَلَيْهِ وَسَلَّمَ said: "Do not revile my Companions, do not revile my Companions. By Him in whose hand is my soul, even if one of you were to spend a mountain of gold, he would not reach the status of any of them, or even halfway." Al-Tirmidhī, 3862 also narrated that the Prophet صَلَّى ٱللَّهُ عَلَيْهِ وَسَلَّمَ said, "Be careful with my Companions: do not make them targets after me. Anyone who loves them loves them through love of me; anyone who hates them hates them through hatred of me. To offend them is to offend me, and to offend me is to offend God; and the one who offends God draws ever closer to being taken to task by Him."

49 This is a reference to Qurʾān 5:54.

piety,[50] knowledge, competence, and kinship to Quraysh; the latter because the Prophet ﷺ said, "The *imāms* are from Quraysh."[51] If there are several candidates who all meet these criteria, the *imām* is the one to whom most people pledge their allegiance. Anyone who opposes this majority is a rebel who must be brought back to allegiance to the truth.

The tenth foundation: If the one who occupies the *imāma* is not possessed of piety and knowledge, but opposition to him would inevitably lead to civil strife, then we must consider his *imāma* valid. This is [true] because in such a situation we would only have two possible alternatives: One would be to stir up civil strife in seeking to supplant him, which would bring the Muslims more harm than what they would have suffered [from] the absence of these conditions [of piety and knowledge in the *imām*]. These conditions were established because they are complementary to the public welfare (*maṣlaḥa*), and obsession with things that are complementary to the public welfare must never be allowed to destroy that welfare itself. That would be like destroying a city to build a palace. The other alternative would be to rule that the land has no *imām* at all and that all legal processes are invalid. This is inconceivable. If we acknowledge the authority of the iniquitous in their own lands because it is an unavoidable necessity for [the people of that land], then why should we not acknowledge the legitimacy of the *imāma* when there is a need and necessity for it?

These, then, are the four pillars containing forty fundamentals which together constitute the principles of the creed. He who believes in them is in accordance with the people of the *sunna* and distinct from the heretics.

---

50 "By piety (*warʿ*) he means suitability (*ʿadāla*), which is the more common expression." Al-Zabīdī, *Itḥāf*, 2:230.

51 Al-Nasāʾī, 5909.

May God تَعَالَىٰ strengthen us with success through His grace, and guide us to the truth and to realization of it through His bounty, munificence, and favor. May God bless our master Muḥammad, his family, and every servant He has chosen.

4

On Faith (*Īmān*) and Islam, What Connects and Separates Them, Whether Faith Can Increase and Decrease, and Whether the Predecessors Qualified Their Claims to Faith [by Saying "God Willing"]

This chapter comprises three subjects of inquiry.

[Is Islam Identical with Faith (*īmān*), or Distinct from it?]

THE [scholars] have differed as to whether Islam is identical with faith, or distinct from it; and if it is distinct from it, then is [faith] so separate from it that it can exist without [Islam], or is [faith] connected to [Islam] and a concomitant of it. Some say that they are the same thing, others that they are two separate things, and still others that they are two things but that one is connected to the other. Abū Ṭālib al-Makkī spoke on this matter at great length and complexity,[1] but let us instead go directly to the heart of the matter without digressing into unhelpful details.

We say, then, that this discussion comprises three considerations: a consideration of the lexical meaning of the two words, a consideration of their meaning when used by revelation (*al-sharʿ*), [lit., the law], and a consideration of their ruling with respect to this life and the hereafter. The first study is linguistic, the second exegetical, and the third juristic and legalistic.

1 Abū Ṭālib al-Makkī, *Qūt al-qulūb*, 2:129.

The First Consideration: The Requisite of Language

The truth about this is that faith (*īmān*) means belief (*taṣdīq*). God تَعَالَى says, *But you will not have faith* [bi-mu'min] *in us* [12:17]; that is, you will not believe (*bi-muṣadiq*) us. Islam means submission and surrender with obedience and compliance, and to renounce all rebellion, refusal, and obstinacy.

Belief is housed in a specific place, namely the heart, and the tongue is its interpreter. As for submission, it covers the heart, tongue, and the rest of the body. To believe with the heart is to submit and renounce rebellion and disavowal in every case, and likewise to acknowledge with the tongue, and to obey and comply with the rest of the body.

Thus according to the requisite of language, Islam is more general and faith is more specific. Faith is, as it were, an expression for the noblest part of Islam. All belief is submission, but not every submission is belief.

The Second Consideration: Their Application in the Law

The truth is that when these terms are applied by the law sometimes they are used as synonyms in succession, other times they are distinct, and still other times they are interconnected.

Their use as synonyms can be found in God's words, *So We brought out whoever was in the cities of the believers. And We found not within them other than a* [*single*] *house of muslims*[2] [51:35–36]. There is consensus that there was only a single household of them. Again, God says [Moses says to his people:] *if you have believed in God, then rely upon Him, if you should be muslims*[3] [10:84]. The

2 That is, those who submit (*muslimīn*).

3 That is, those who submit (*muslimīn*).This refers to Moses.

Prophet ﷺ said, "Islam was built upon five [pillars],"[4] and on another occasion gave these five pillars as a definition for faith.[5]

Their use as distinct terms can be found in God's words, *The bedouins say, "We have believed* (āmannā)." *Say, "You have not* [*yet*] *believed; but say* [*instead*], '*We have submitted* (*aslamnā*)'" [49:14]. That is, "We have submitted outwardly." By faith here is meant the belief of the heart alone, and by submission is meant the outward submission of the tongue and body.

Consider also the *ḥadīth* of Gabriel عَلَيْهِ السَّلَامُ and how, when he asked about faith, the Prophet answered, "It is to believe in God, His angels, His books, His messengers, the Last Day, the resurrection after death, the reckoning, and predestination, the good and the bad of it." Then he said, "What is Islam?" and he answered with the five pillars,[6] thereby defining Islam as outward submission through word and deed.

Consider also the *ḥadīth* [transmitted by] Saʿd رَضِيَ اللَّهُ عَنْهُ describing how the Prophet ﷺ gave something to one man and not to another. Saʿd رَضِيَ اللَّهُ عَنْهُ said to him, "O Messenger of God, you ignored so-and-so and did not give anything to him, but he is a believer." He ﷺ replied, "Or a Muslim?" Saʿd رَضِيَ اللَّهُ عَنْهُ repeated what he had said, and the Messenger of God ﷺ did the same.[7]

Their use as interconnected terms can be found in the narration recounting how the Prophet was asked, "Which action is best?" He ﷺ replied, "Islam." The questioner said, "Then which Islam is best?" He ﷺ said, "Faith."[8]

This shows how words are used as distinct terms and also as interconnected terms. The latter is the most useful lexical usage,[9] because faith is an action and indeed the best of actions, while Islam means submission either with the heart, the tongue, or the body; and the best of these is submission with the heart, which means

---

4 Al-Bukhārī, 8; and Muslim, 16.

5 Al-Bayhaqī, *al-Sunan al-kubrā*, 4:199, and also without mention of the pilgrimage by al-Bukhārī, 53; and Muslim, 17.

6 Muslim, 8. See also the editor's introduction to the present book, xxii–xxiii.

7 Al-Bukhārī, 27; and Muslim, 150.

8 Aḥmad b. Ḥanbal, *Musnad*, 4:114.

9 That is, its occurrence in the context of interconnectedness is the most useful example in the language, see al-Zabīdī, *Itḥāf*, 2:239.

belief, also called faith. Now the use of the two words as distinct terms, interconnected terms, or synonyms are all valid uses that do not go beyond the lexical meanings of the words.

Their use as distinct terms means that faith becomes an expression of belief in the heart only, which accords with the lexical meaning, and that Islam becomes an expression of outward submission, which also accords with the lexical meaning. To submit partially is still legitimately called submission, for it is not necessary that a word's meaning be exhaustively realized in every possible way in order for it to be used correctly. It is sufficient to touch something with part of one's body in order to be described as "touching" it; one need not touch it with one's entire body in order for the word to be valid. Likewise, to use the word "Islam" to describe outward submission, even when there is no inward submission, is a valid use of the word. This is the meaning of God's words, *The bedouins say, "We have believed* (āmannā)." *Say, "You have not [yet] believed; but say [instead], 'We have submitted* (aslamnā)' [49:14] and the words of the Prophet ﷺ in the *ḥadīth* of Saʿd, "Or a Muslim?" because he preferred one of them to the other and used the words in distinct senses to indicate which of the two is superior.

Their use as interconnected terms also accords with the lexical meaning of the specificity of faith: it is to make Islam an expression of submission with heart, word, and deed all together, and faith an expression of part of what Islam entails, namely belief in the heart. This is what we mean by "interconnection," and it accords with the lexical meaning of faith as a specific term and Islam as a general term. This explains why he answered the question "What Islam is best?" by saying, "faith." He made faith a specific aspect of Islam, thus including it within it.

As for their use as synonyms, this makes Islam an expression of submission both in the heart and outwardly, since all this is submission. The same happens with [the meaning of faith], its specificity is broadened so that it includes outward expressions in its meaning. This is lexically valid because outward submission in word and deed is the fruit of inner belief. The name of a tree can be used liberally to mean both the tree and its fruit. In this manner of generalization, faith becomes a synonym for the term Islam with the same implications, neither adding to it nor subtracting from it. This is how the terms are used in God's words, *and We found not within them other than a* [*single*] *house of muslims* [51:36].

The Third Consideration: The Legal Ruling

ISLAM and faith have two rulings, one pertaining to this life and the other to the hereafter. The ruling pertaining to the hereafter is that they bring one out of hell and save one from abiding there eternally. The Messenger of God ﷺ said, "Anyone with a mustard seed of faith in his heart will come out of the fire."[10] The scholars have differed as to the exact nature of this ruling, [as it] depends on what exactly faith is. Some say that faith is simply confirmation (*ʿaqd*),[11] others that it is confirmation in the heart and testimony with the tongue,[12] still others that it means to practice the pillars of Islam.[13]

[FIRST,] in order to shed light on the truth of this matter, let us say that all [the scholars] agree that anyone who attains all three of these will have a place in paradise. This is the first level.

THE SECOND LEVEL [involves] attaining the first two and part of the third, that is, verbalizing, confirming, and performing some righteous actions but also committing one or more major sins. The Muʿtazila say that such a person has lost his faith, but has not actually become a disbeliever, and is called an evildoer (*fāsiq*), [so he] occupies a position between the two, and he will abide in hell forever. This is false, as we shall explain.

---

10 Al-Bukhārī, 22; Muslim, 183; and al-Tirmidhī, 2598.

11 "This is the preference of the Ashʿarīs and the view of the Māturīdīs." Al-Zabīdī, *Itḥāf*, 2:241.

12 "This has been attributed to Abū Ḥanīfa and is the dominant view of his followers, as well as certain men of insight (*muḥaqqiqīn*) among the Ashʿarīs." Al-Zabīdī, *Itḥāf*, 2:241.

13 "This is the position of the Khawārij, which is what made them declare all sinners disbelievers, because there is no conceivable middle ground between disbelief and faith." Al-Zabīdī, *Itḥāf*, 2:242.

THE THIRD LEVEL is to believe with the heart and testify with the tongue without performing any righteous acts with the body. The scholars have differed on the ruling for such a person.

Abū Ṭālib al-Makkī said that bodily acts are part of faith and that it is incomplete without them, and he claimed that there is consensus on this point, citing evidence that actually works against him, such as God's words, *those who believe and do righteous deeds* [2:25, and others], because this actually implies that acts come after faith and are not part of it, as otherwise it would be needless repetition to mention acts. Neither is his claim of consensus credible, as he himself related the Prophet's صَلَّىٱللَّهُعَلَيْهِوَسَلَّمَ words "No one disbelieves unless he denies what I have affirmed"[14] and criticized the Muʿtazila for their view that those who commit major sins will abide in hell forever.[15]

Actually, the one who holds this view is no different from the Muʿtazila because if it were said to him, "If someone believes with his heart and testifies with his tongue and then dies right then, will he go to paradise?" he would be obliged to answer yes, which is an affirmation that faith can exist without acts. We would ask him then, "What if he were to remain alive long enough to miss a single prayer, and then die, or if he were to commit adultery and then die—would he abide in hell forever?" If he says yes, then this is exactly what the Muʿtazila say. If he says no, this would be a clear admission that acts are not an integral part of faith itself, nor a condition of its existence, nor what makes it worthy of paradise.

He might say, "I meant that this applies if he were to live a long time without praying or performing any acts [of worship]." To this, we would say, "What determines how long this period should be? How many acts does he need to neglect before his faith is annulled? How many major sins does he need to commit before his faith is annulled?" This is not something that can be specified, and no one has ever clarified it.

THE FOURTH LEVEL is to believe with the heart and then die before testifying with the tongue or performing any acts. Should we say that such a person is a believer whose faith is between him

14 Al-Ṭabarānī, *al-Muʿjam al-awsaṭ*, 4430.

15 Abū Ṭālib al-Makkī, *Qūt al-qulūb*, 2:130–131.

and God تَعَالَىٰ?[16] This is a matter of dispute. Those who stipulate that testimony is required to make faith complete would say that such a person has died before having faith. However, this is false because the Prophet صَلَّىٱللَّهُعَلَيْهِوَسَلَّمَ said anyone with a mustard seed of faith in his heart will come out of the fire, and this person's heart is filled with faith, so how could he abide in hell forever? Also, the *ḥadīth* of Gabriel عَلَيْهِٱلسَّلَامُ does not stipulate anything for faith aside from belief in God تَعَالَىٰ and His angels, His books, His messengers, and the Last Day, [and predestination] as we saw earlier.

The fifth level is to believe with the heart and have enough time to proclaim the testimonies of faith, and know its obligations, but not to have [time to] actually express it. Here it is possible to say that such a person's failure to proclaim the testimonies is similar to his failure to pray. We would say that he is a believer and will not abide in the fire forever; faith is purely belief, and the tongue is the interpreter for faith. Therefore faith must already exist in a complete form before the tongue can give voice to it. This is the more obvious interpretation because we can only rely on the lexical meanings of the words, and the lexical meaning of faith is belief with the heart. The Prophet صَلَّىٱللَّهُعَلَيْهِوَسَلَّمَ said that anyone with a mustard seed of faith in his heart will come out of the fire, and faith cannot be removed entirely from the heart simply by the failure to make the obligatory proclamation any more than it can be removed by the failure to perform obligatory actions.

Others have said that mere proclamation is a pillar because the testimonies of faith do not simply express what is in the heart but rather constitute another conviction and initiate a new testimony and commitment. However, the first explanation is the more obvious one. The Murjiʾa sect went to extremes in this and said that such a person will not enter the fire at all, and that no believer will enter the fire no matter what sins he may commit.[17] We shall refute this claim of theirs presently.

---

16 This is based on the idea that assent by the heart is sufficient for comprehending faith, see al-Zabīdī, *Itḥāf*, 2:245.

17 Their statement is well known: "Disobedience does no harm to someone of faith just as obedience gives no benefit to someone of disbelief."

THE SIXTH LEVEL is to say with the tongue, "There is no god but God and Muḥammad is the messenger of God" while not believing this with the heart. We do not doubt that in the hereafter such a person will be numbered among the disbelievers and will abide in the fire forever. Nor do we doubt that in the case of the ruling for this world as discharged by rulers and governors, he is counted as a Muslim because his heart cannot be read, and we must assume that what he said with his tongue was an expression of what is in his heart. What we are uncertain about, however, is a third matter, namely how the ruling of this world applies to what is between him and God تَعَالَىٰ. Suppose that while he is in this state, a Muslim relative of his dies and then he comes to believe with his heart, and he asks for a legal ruling, saying, "I did not believe with my heart when he died, yet I inherited from him. Is the inheritance [truly] lawful for me [or will it come] between me and God تَعَالَىٰ [on the day of reckoning]?" Or suppose he married a Muslim woman and then came to believe with his heart—does he have to renew his marriage?

This is a matter of debate. It could be said that the laws of this world are based on outward statements without regard to inner states, or it could be said that they are based on outward statements when they involve other people because they cannot see the person's inner state, although his inner state is known to him in those things between himself and God تَعَالَىٰ.

The most obvious position to take—and God knows best—is that this inheritance would be forbidden for him and that he would have to renew his marriage. This is why Ḥudhayfa رَضِيَ ٱللَّهُ عَنْهُ did not attend the funerals of the hypocrites, and ʿUmar رَضِيَ ٱللَّهُ عَنْهُ paid attention to this and did not attend if Ḥudhayfa رَضِيَ ٱللَّهُ عَنْهُ did not attend.[18] Although prayer is an act of worship, it is still an outward action in this world, and keeping away from what is forbidden is also something that God made obligatory just as prayer is obligatory. The Prophet صَلَّى ٱللَّهُ عَلَيْهِ وَسَلَّمَ said, "Seeking what is lawful is another obligation after the obligatory prayer."[19] This does not contradict our assertion that inheritance is based on Islamic law; [Islam] is

18 Wakīʿ, *al-Zuhd*, 477; and Ibn ʿAsākir, *Tārīkh Dimashq*, 12:276.

19 Al-Ṭabarānī, *al-Muʿjam al-kabīr*, 10:74.

submission, indeed complete submission means to submit both inwardly and outwardly.

That said, these are speculative legal discussions based on the outward import of words, generalities, and analogies. It is not appropriate for someone deficient in these sciences to think that the pursuit is for certainty in the customary sense of obtaining [rulings], whereas the field of theology [is about the] pursuit of certainty. No success will come from attempting to follow conventional formalities in the sciences.

You might ask, "What are the doubts raised by the Muʿtazila and Murjiʾa, and what are the proofs that what they say is false?" My answer is that their doubts are raised from certain general verses[20] of the Qurʾān. The Murjiʾa say that no believer will enter the fire even if he is guilty of every sin imaginable because God عَزَّوَجَلَّ says, *whoever believes in his Lord will not fear deprivation or burden* [72:13], and says, *those who have believed in God and His messengers—those are* [*in the ranks of*] *the supporters of truth* [57:19]. They also cite His words, *every time a company is thrown into it, its keepers ask them, "Did there not come to you a warner?" They will say, "Yes, a warner had come to us, but we denied and said, God has not sent down anything. You are not but in great error"* [67:8–9], and say that the general import of the words, *every time a company is thrown into it* is that every company cast into the fire is composed entirely of people who belied revelation. They also point to His words, *none will* [*enter to*] *burn therein except the most wretched one who had denied and turned away* [92:15–16], on the grounds that the negation and affirmation implies that it is exhaustive. Again they cite His words, *whoever comes* [*at judgment*] *with a good deed will have better than it, and they, from the terror of that Day, will be safe* [27:89], on the grounds that faith is the chief of all good deeds. They also cite His words, *God loves the doers of good* [3:148] and, *We will not allow to be lost the reward of any who did well in deeds* [18:30].

Yet none of this constitutes any convincing evidence for their position, because when faith is mentioned in these verses it means faith alongside action; we demonstrated earlier that "faith" when

20 That is, verses that are not specific to an event or law.

used in an absolute sense can mean "Islam," meaning obedience with heart, word, and deed. The evidence for this interpretation is provided by many reports about how sinners will be punished and the duration of their punishment, as well as the Prophet's ﷺ words, "Anyone with a mustard seed of faith in his heart will come out of the fire." How could they come out if they never went in?

A proof from the Qurʾān is found in God's words, *God does not forgive association with Him, but He forgives what is less than that for whom He wills* [4:48]. This qualification, depending on His will, indicates that there is a division.[21] Again, God says, *and whoever disobeys God and His Messenger—then indeed, for him is the fire of hell* [72:23]; to state that this refers to disbelief only is simply arbitrary. Consider also His words, *unquestionably, the wrongdoers are in an enduring punishment* [42:45], *and whoever comes with an evil deed—their faces will be overturned into the fire* [27:90].

So these are some general verses to counter those that they cited. We must apply specificity and interpretation to both sides because the reports plainly state that sinners will be punished;[22] indeed, God's words, *and there is none of you except he will come to it* [19:71] seem to state that this will be inevitable for everyone because no believer is entirely innocent of sin.[23] When He تَعَالَىٰ says *none shall*

21 "That is, a division into major sins and minor sins. It implies that even minor sins can be punished regardless of whether or not the one who committed them avoided major sins, because of God's words, *What is this book that leaves nothing small or great except that it has enumerated it?* [18:49]; and this record could only be for the purpose of reckoning and requital." Al-Zabīdī, *Itḥāf*, 2:251.

22 Something similar is reported by al-Bukhārī, 7450, the Prophet said, "Various peoples will be afflicted by a scorching fire as a punishment because of the sins they committed. Then God will cause them to enter the garden by the graciousness of His mercy. They will be addressed as, 'people of hell' (*al-jahannamiyyūn*)."

23 "The passage over the traverse [over hell to paradise] is the way by which all people will 'come to' the fire. This is how this verse was interpreted by Ibn Masʿūd, al-Ḥasan, and Qatāda. God follows this verse by saying, *then We will save those who feared God and leave the wrongdoers within it, on their knees* (19:72). Some people interpret "come to it" to mean "enter in," as in the *ḥadīth* of Jābir, that the Prophet said, 'Everyone, righteous or iniquitous, will enter it, except that for the believers it will be cool and peaceful as it was for Abraham, such that the fire will cry out at their coolness, *Then We shall save those who were conscious* [*of Us*]..." Narrated by Aḥmad b. Ḥanbal, Ibn Abī Shayba, ʿAbd b. Ḥumayd, Abū Yaʿlā, al-Nasāʾī in *al-Kinā*, al-Bayhaqī, and others. It is sound (*ḥasan*)." Al-Zabīdī, *Itḥāf*, 2:251.

be roasted in it but the wretched [92:15] He means a specific group of people, or possibly one specific person. When He says *every time a company is thrown into it* [67:8], He means a company of disbelievers. Thus it is an easy matter to apply specificity to general texts. It was because of this verse that al-Ashʿarī and several other theologians took the position that general texts must not be taken literally, and that judgment should be suspended on such phrases until other textual evidence can be found to contextualize them and show their true meaning.

As for the Muʿtazila, they raised their doubts by citing God's words, *but indeed, I am the [perpetual] Forgiver of whoever repents and believes and does righteousness* [20:82]; *By time, indeed, mankind is in loss, except for those who have believed and done righteous deeds* [103:1–3]; *And there is none of you except he will come to it. This is upon your Lord an inevitability decreed* [19:71], and then immediately after: *Then We will save those who feared God* [19:72]; *And whoever disobeys God and His Messenger—then indeed, for him is the fire of hell* [72:23]. They also cite every verse wherein righteous action is linked with faith. Then there are God's words, *whoever kills a believer intentionally—his recompense is hell, wherein he will abide eternally* [4:93].

Again, these general texts are given specificity by others, which is proven by God's statement, *He forgives what is less than that for whom He wills* [4:48], thus it is appropriate that the will remains always with Him to forgive anything but the association of partners with Him. Likewise, we again refer to the Prophet's صَلَّى ٱللَّٰهُ عَلَيْهِ وَسَلَّمَ words, "Anyone with a mustard seed of faith in his heart will come out of the fire," and to God's words *We will not allow to be lost the reward of any who did well in deeds* [18:30], and *God does not allow to be lost the reward of the doers of good* [9:120]. How, then, could He allow both faith itself and all other good deeds to be lost on account of a single sin? As for His words *whoever kills a believer intentionally* [4:93], this refers to killing a believer because of his faith; there was a specific incident connected to the revelation of this verse.[24]

24 This verse was revealed after a man accepted blood-money from his brother's murderer and then apostatized, killed the murderer, and fled to Mecca. Thus the punishment in the verse refers to his apostasy. Al-Suyūṭī, *al-Durr al-manthūr*, 2:622.

You might say, "It appears that you incline to the view that faith can exist even without action. Yet it is well-known that the predecessors used to say that faith means belief, word, and deed—what does this mean?"

To this, our answer is that it is not unlikely that action is considered a part of faith because it completes it and perfects it, just as it can be said that the head and hands are part of a human being, although a man ceases to be a man when he loses his head, but not so when he loses his hand. Likewise, the formulas of glorification (*tasbīḥāt*) and the refrain "God is Great" (*Allāh akbar*) can be called part of the prayer even though [prayer] is not invalidated if they are omitted.

Belief with the heart is to faith what the head is to a man: it cannot exist without it. The other good deeds are like the limbs, some of them higher than others. The Prophet صَلَّى ٱللَّٰهُ عَلَيْهِ وَسَلَّمَ said, "The adulterer is not a believer in the moment when he commits adultery."[25] The Companions رَضِيَ ٱللَّٰهُ عَنْهُمْ did not believe, as the Muʿtazila do, that adultery takes a person beyond the faith;[26] rather, what it means is that such a person is not a true believer with complete and perfect faith; similarly one might say that an incapacitated person with dismembered limbs is "not a person" in the sense that he does not have the perfection of form that represents the human ideal.[27]

Inquiry [On the Increase and Decrease of Faith]

You might say, "The predecessors agreed that faith increases and decreases: acts of obedience increase it, and sins decrease it. Yet if faith means faith, then it seems inconceivable that it could increase or decrease."

---

25 Al-Bukhārī, 2475; and Muslim, 57.

26 That is, they believed that the adulterer is no longer a Muslim.

27 Abū Ṭālib al-Makkī commented on this *ḥadīth*: "There is a subtle meaning in this *ḥadīth*, which is that a person in this state has relinquished his faith [that comes from] modesty, and the Prophet صَلَّى ٱللَّٰهُ عَلَيْهِ وَسَلَّمَ said, 'Modesty is part of faith.' The modest person does not unclothe himself for any unlawful purpose, and he remains a believer in Islam, [God's] unity, and the rulings of the law." Abū Ṭālib al-Makkī, *Qūt al-qulūb*, 2:132.

In answer to this, I say that the predecessors were righteous witnesses, and there is no justification in deviating from their stance. What they said is true; it is only a matter of understanding it. [The saying of the predecessors] actually indicates that action is not an integral part of faith and a pillar of its existence, but rather an addition to it. An addition can exist, and a deficiency can exist, but the thing itself does not increase. One cannot say that a man gains an addition from [the existence of] his head, but one could very well say that he gains an addition through his beard and weight. Again, one could not say that prayer increases through bowing and prostrating, but one can say that it increases through matters of correct conduct (*ādāb*) and voluntary actions (*sunan*). This clearly illustrates how faith has its own being, and that beyond this existence, its state can change through increase and decrease.

You might say, "The problem remains: how can belief increase and decrease when it is a single quality?"

In answer to this, I say that if we set aside the dissimulation and [we are] not be concerned with stirring up conflict, we can solve this problem. Let us say, then, that faith is a word with several meanings that amount to three different usages:

First, it is used to mean belief with the heart in the sense of conviction and blind imitation (*taqlīd*) without any direct disclosure or expansion of the breast. This is the faith of the common folk, indeed of all mankind save for the elite. This conviction is a knot in the heart: sometimes it is tight and strong, other times loose and weak, just like a knot in a piece of string.

Do not find this far-fetched, but rather consider how firm the Jew can be in his creed, such that you cannot talk him out of it whether by warning him and inspiring fear in him, counseling him and exhorting him to reflect, nor offering him proofs and rational arguments. Consider also Christians and heretics, some of whom can be driven to doubt with the simplest of words, and persuaded to renounce their convictions with the lightest of inducements or warnings even though, like the Jew, they have no doubt in their doctrines. The difference between them is the level of determination. This also applies to true conviction.

Acts cause this determination to develop and grow, just as watering plants causes them to grow. This is why God تَعَالَىٰ says, *but it [merely] increased them in faith* [3:173], and *it [a sūra] increased them in faith* [9:124], and *that they would increase in faith along with their [present] faith* [48:4].

The Prophet صَلَّىٰ ٱللَّٰهُ عَلَيْهِ وَسَلَّمَ is related to have said, "Faith increases and decreases." This is so because of the effect of acts of obedience on the heart. This can only be perceived by one who observes the differing states of his soul at those times when he is engaged in worship, and when he focuses on them with presence of heart at those times of quietude, and he perceives variations in tranquility, as related to the doctrines of faith concerning these states, so that his conviction increases as protection from those who seek to loosen it by inspiring doubt in him. As such, if someone is convinced that the meaning of mercy as related to orphans is to act according to the necessity of his conviction then when he acts on his belief and pats an orphan's head and treats him kindly, he will have an inner experience confirming this mercy and multiplying [his belief] because of his action. Likewise, if someone is convinced that humility means acting according to the necessity of this by serving or bowing to someone, he will feel humility in his heart when he performs this service.

The same is true for the other qualities of the heart concerning bodily acts that arise from them. Thus the effects of these acts return to them, confirming and increasing them. This will be seen in the Quarter of Perils and Deliverance [of the *Iḥyāʾ*] (*Rubʿ al-munjiyāt wa-l-muhlikāt*) when we explain how the inner state is connected to the outer, and how acts are connected to beliefs and hearts. This is an aspect of how the worldly kingdom is connected to the realm of spiritual dominance; by "worldly kingdom" (*mulk*) I mean the visible world perceived by the senses, and by "realm of spiritual dominance" (*malakūt*) I mean the world of the unseen (*ghayb*) perceived by the light of insight. The heart is from the realm of spiritual dominance, while the bodily limbs and their deeds are from the worldly kingdom. The connection between these two realms is so subtle and fine that some have imagined that they are identical. Others have imagined that the only world that exists is the visible one, composed of these tangible bodies. Someone who perceives both matters and then perceives their plurality and their connectedness is described by this saying:

> The glass is transparent and so is the wine;
> They appear alike, and hence the confusion:
>
> There seems to be wine and no glass;
> There seems to be glass and no wine.[28]

Let us return to the matter at hand, as this was a digression outside the science of practical conduct. However, the two sciences are also related and connected, which is why you will see the sciences of disclosure constantly intruding on the sciences of practical conduct, until you have to make a conscious effort to hold them back.

This, then, is the sense in which faith can increase through obedience, as in the following. ʿAlī [may God ennoble his face] therefore said,

> Faith begins as a white dot, and when the servant does righteous deeds it grows until the entire heart is white. Hypocrisy begins as a black dot, and when he indulges in forbidden things it grows until the entire heart is black, covered by it. This is what it means for the heart to be sealed.

Then he recited God's words, *No! Rather, the stain has covered their hearts* [83:14].[29]

THE SECOND USAGE of the word "faith" is belief and action together, as is the case in the Prophet's صَلَّى ٱللَّٰهُ عَلَيْهِ وَسَلَّمَ words, "Faith has seventy something doors"[30] and his words, "The adulterer is not a believer in the moment when he commits adultery." When action is included in the meaning of faith, it is clear how it can increase and decrease. What is subject to debate is whether this results in an increase in faith in the sense of belief alone; as we indicated earlier, it does affect this.

---

28 The lines were composed by Ibn ʿAbbād, 176.

29 Abū Ṭālib al-Makkī, *Qūt al-qulūb*, 2:135. Al-Bayhaqī narrated something similar in *Shuʿab al-īmān*, 37.

30 Al-Tirmidhī, 2614; and by al-Bukhārī, 9; and Muslim, 35 with "branches" instead of "doors."

THE THIRD USAGE of the word is certain belief by way of disclosure, the expansion of the breast, and witnessing by the light of insight. Of all of them, this is the one furthest from the possibility of increase. However, I say that when it comes to matters of certitude wherein there is no doubt, the tranquility of the soul (*ṭumaʾnīnat al-nafs*) differs concerning each matter. The certainty of the soul that two is greater than one is not the same as its certainty that the world is created and contingent, even though it does not doubt in either one. This is [true] because objects of certitude differ in clarity, and thus the soul's tranquility in them [differs as well]. We touched on this in the section [entitled] "Scholars of the hereafter and certitude" in *The Book of Knowledge* in chapter 6: "The Perils of [the pursuit of] knowledge: An elucidation of the traits of the scholars of the hereafter," so there is no need to repeat it here.

After examining these usages, it is clear that what they said about the increase and decrease of faith is true. How could it be otherwise, when the report tells us that "Anyone with a mustard seed of faith in his heart will come out of the fire," or in another version "a dinar's worth."[31] What meaning could these different measures of worth have, if faith were simply a designation of the heart and had no levels?

Inquiry [Is it Acceptable to Say, "I am a Believer, God Willing"]

YOU might ask about the proper way to understand the saying of the predecessors, "I am a believer, God willing," when this qualification is an expression of doubt, and doubting faith is equivalent to disbelief. When asked about their faith, [the predecessors] would all avoid giving a simple affirmative answer, and [they would] be careful about this. Sufyān al-Thawrī رَحِمَهُ ٱللَّٰهُ said, "Whoever says, 'I am a believer in God's sight,' is a liar, and whoever says, 'I am a true believer,' has [uttered] an innovation (*fa-huwa bidʿa*)."[32] But why is he a liar, when he knows himself that

31 Al-Bukhārī, 7440; and Muslim, 183.

32 Abū Ṭālib al-Makkī, *Qūt al-qulūb*, 2:137.

he is a believer? Anyone who knows himself to be a believer must be a believer in God's sight, just as anyone who knows himself to be tall or generous must be so in God's sight, and the same [is true with regard to] being happy or sad, or possessed of hearing or sight. If someone were asked, "Are you an animal?" he would not happily say, "I am an animal if God wills."

When Sufyān made this statement, someone said to him, "What should we say then?"

He replied, "Say, 'We believe in God and in what He has sent down to us.'" Yet what is the difference between saying "We believe in God and in what He has sent down to us" and saying, "I am a believer?"

Again, Ḥasan was asked, "Are you a believer?"

He replied, "God willing."

Someone said to him, "O Abū Saʿīd, did you qualify your own faith?"

He said, "I fear that if I were to say yes, God would say, 'You lie, Ḥasan,' and that would seal my fate."

He also used to say, "How can I be sure that God سُبْحَانَهُ has not seen me do something displeasing to Him, and abhorred me for it and said, 'Be on your way, for I shall accept no deed of yours,' and that I am not toiling in vain?"

Ibrāhīm [al-Nakhaʿī][33] said, "If you are asked if you are a believer, say, 'There is no god but God.'"

Another time he said, "Say, 'I do not doubt in faith, but your questioning me about it is a heretical innovation.'"

ʿAlqama was asked, "Are you are believer?"

He replied, "I hope so, God willing."

[Sufyān] al-Thawrī said, "We are believers in God, His angels, His books, and His messengers. We do not know what we are in God's sight."[34]

What, then, do all these qualifications mean?[35]

---

33 This is Ibn Yazīd al-Nakhaʿī, the jurist of Kufa. He is not Ibn Adham, see al-Zabīdī, *Itḥāf*, 2:264.

34 Abū Ṭālib al-Makkī, *Qūt al-qulūb*, 2:137.

35 Although some people established that the righteous predecessors made this qualification, another group, namely the Ḥanafīs, refuted that. One example is

The answer is that this qualification is valid, and has four justifications: two pertain to doubt, not in faith itself, but in its final end or its perfection; the other two do not pertain to doubt at all.

THE FIRST JUSTIFICATION [that] does not pertain to doubt is the desire to avoid a confident claim [to faith] out of fear that it is a [way of claiming] self-purification (*min tazkiyat al-nafs*). God تَعَالَىٰ says, *so do not claim yourselves to be pure* [53:32], and again, *have you not seen those who claim themselves to be pure? ... Look how they invent untruths about God* [4:49–50].

A wise man was asked, "When is the truth ugly?" He replied, "When a man praises himself." Faith is one of the noblest attributes, and to make a confident claim to it is an act of praising oneself. Therefore, formulating a qualification to it is following the conventional way of praising oneself, just as when, if a person is asked if he is a doctor, or jurist, or exegete, he might say, "Yes, God willing." This is not to cast doubt on the matter, but rather to avoid praising oneself.

This type of formulation suggests a reexamination and a questioning of the soundness of the essential claim (*al-tardīd wa-l-taḍʿīf li-nafs al-khabar*),[36] but the meaning of it is to lessen a particular implication of the claim, namely praising oneself. According to this interpretation, if one were asked about a negative attribute, it would not be right to make this qualification.

---

the narration stating that Ibn ʿUmar رَضِيَ اللَّهُ عَنْهُمَا brought out a ram for slaughter, and took it to a man, to whom he said, "Are you a believer?" He replied, "Yes, God willing." Ibn ʿUmar رَضِيَ اللَّهُ عَنْهُمَا said, "A man who doubts his faith is not fit to slaughter my sacrifice." It is also related that ʿAṭāʾ used to criticize those who qualified their faith, and that Ibn Masʿūd رَضِيَ اللَّهُ عَنْهُ prayed for forgiveness after he inadvertently did so while debating with a companion of Muʿādh b. Jabal رَضِيَ اللَّهُ عَنْهُ. There are many other examples. It may be that [al-Ghazālī رَحِمَهُ اللَّهُ] went to these lengths to shed light on this issue because of the extreme lengths to which certain Ḥanafīs went in holding to their position, to the extent of leveling accusations of disbelief and misguidance against those who disagreed. As Taqī l-Dīn al-Subkī said, it is a marginal issue that does not require such vehement disagreement. Al-Zabīdī said in *Itḥāf*, 2:265, "Our Ḥanafī scholars have expounded on this matter at great length, but I have declined to detail this here because of the accusations of disbelief, misguidance, and lawlessness that much of it contains, which made me prefer not to include it." See also al-Zabīdī, *Itḥāf*, 2:281.

36 According to the linguistic meaning, the use of "if" [in the phrase "if God wills"] includes a sense of doubt. It necessitates a questioning of the soundness of the essential statement.

The second justification is the desire to adhere to the praiseworthy trait of mentioning God تَعَالَىٰ at all times and consigning all things to God's will. God تَعَالَىٰ taught His Prophet صَلَّىٰ ٱللَّٰهُ عَلَيْهِ وَسَلَّمَ, *and never say of anything, "Indeed, I will do that tomorrow," except* [*when adding*], *"if God wills"* [18:23–24]. He did not limit this to such things [that are doubtful] but also [meant it] for that wherein there is no doubt, for He said, *you will surely enter al-Masjid al-Ḥarām, if God wills, in safety, with your heads shaved and* [*hair*] *shortened* [48:27]. Of course God سُبْحَانَهُ knew that they would enter, and He had willed it so, but His purpose was to teach [the Prophet] this. The Messenger of God صَلَّىٰ ٱللَّٰهُ عَلَيْهِ وَسَلَّمَ followed this conduct whenever he spoke of things to come, whether they were certain or doubtful, even to the extent [that he] said, when he entered graveyards, "Peace be upon you, people of faith. God willing, we will follow you."[37] There was no doubt that he would follow them [to death], but good conduct demands that God عَزَّ وَجَلَّ be mentioned and that all things be consigned to Him, and this expression achieves this.[38] Eventually it became a conventional phrase for expressing desire and hope, so that if someone were to say to you, "So-and-so will die soon," and you replied, "God willing," he would think that you were expressing your desire for this, not that you were doubting it would happen.

Again, if [someone] were to say to you, "So-and-so will get better and his illness will be cured," and you replied, "God willing," with the intention of expressing a hope, your words would change from being an expression of doubt to an expression of hope, and also to an expression of good conduct by mentioning God عَزَّ وَجَلَّ at every opportunity.

The third justification, this time pertaining to doubt, is that it means, "I am truly a believer, God willing." God تَعَالَىٰ said of the noble status of certain people, *those are the believers, truly* [8:4]. Thus [the believers] are divided into two groups. This refers to doubt about the perfection of faith, not the basic presence of faith. Every person has doubts about the perfection of his faith, and this does

37 Muslim, 249.

38 The act of saying God willing, "indicates [that one has] the intent to seek [God's] blessing by good conduct. In any case it is a reference to the future, and qualifying a statement about the future is beyond reproach." Al-Zabīdī, *Itḥāf*, 2:266.

not amount to disbelief. Doubting the perfection of one's faith is valid in two senses:

The first is that hypocrisy makes faith imperfect, and is so subtle that no one can ever be certain that he is innocent of it. The second is that faith is perfected by acts of obedience, and their perfection is ever elusive.

As for action, God تَعَالَىٰ says, *the believers are only the ones who have believed in God and His Messenger and then doubt not but strive with their properties and their lives in the cause of God. It is those who are the truthful* [49:15]. Thus what is doubted is the extent of this veracity. Likewise, He says, *but* [*true*] *righteousness is* [*in*] *one who believes in God, and the Last Day* [2:177], there being twenty attributes including honoring covenants and having patience in times of adversity. Then He says, *those are the ones who have been true* [2:177]. Again, He says, *God will raise those who have believed among you and those who were given knowledge* [58:11]; *Not equal among you are those who spent before the conquest* [*of Mecca*] *and fought* [*and those who did so after it*] [57:10]; *They are* [*varying*] *degrees in the sight of God* [3:163]. Then the Prophet صَلَّىٱللَّهُعَلَيْهِوَسَلَّمَ said, "Faith is naked, and its clothing is piety."[39] And again, "Faith has seventy something doors, the lowest of which is to move dangerous objects from the road."[40]

---

39 Ibn Abī Shayba, *al-Muṣannaf*, 36383; and Ibn ʿAsākir, *Tārīkh Dimashq*, 63:389, as a saying of Wahb b. Munabbih. Abū Ṭālib al-Makkī mentioned in *Qūt al-qulūb*, 1:138, "Ḥamza al-Khurāsānī reported it from Sufyān al-Thawrī from ʿAbdallāh, from the Prophet صَلَّىٱللَّهُعَلَيْهِوَسَلَّمَ." It is also reported by al-Khaṭīb al-Baghdādī in *al-Faqīh wa-l-mutafaqqih*, 129–130, as both a saying of the Prophet and a saying of a Companion. Abū Ṭālib said, "We say about this report, 'Faith is naked, its clothing is piety, its embellishment is fear of God, and its fruit is knowledge,' that it contains evidence to show that whoever has no piety has not clothed his faith, and whoever has no fear of God, has not beautifed his faith, and whoever has no knowledge has no fruit from his faith. If he is in accord with ignorance, oppression, and corruption, then he resembles the hypocrites rather than the believers. His faith is nearer to hypocrisy, and his certainty inclines to doubt. He has not been expelled from having the name of faith, it is only that his faith is naked without clothes, stripped with no reward. It is as He says, *or had earned through its faith some good* (6:158). Hypocrisy has various stations, it is said there are seventy doors, and polytheism likewise has numerous levels." Abū Ṭālib al-Makkī, *Qūt al-qulūb*, 2:135

40 Al-Tirmidhī, 2614; and by al-Bukhārī, 9; and Muslim, 35, with "branches" instead of "doors."

The forgoing shows how the perfection of faith is linked to actions. As for how it is linked to innocence from hypocrisy and hidden idolatry (*al-shirk al-khafi*), consider the Prophet's ﷺ words, "If a man has four traits, he is a pure hypocrite even if he fasts, prays, and claims to be a believer: when he speaks, he lies; when he promises, he breaks the promise; when he is trusted, he betrays; when he argues, he deviates from the truth." One narration has, for this last one, "when he makes a covenant, he violates it."[41]

Then there is the *ḥadīth* [transmitted by] Abū Saʿīd al-Khudrī, "There are four kinds of hearts: a pure heart containing a bright light, which is the heart of a believer;[42] a heart that is two-faced, containing faith and hypocrisy…"; the *ḥadīth* goes on to liken faith to an herb nourished by fresh water, and hypocrisy to an abscess nourished by pus; whichever of them dominates in a person will come to define him. Another version has, "whichever of them dominates in a person will take him away."[43]

He ﷺ also said, "Most of the hypocrites of this community will be among the learned."[44] And in another *ḥadīth*, "Idolatry is more hidden in my community than the creeping of an ant over a rock."[45]

Ḥudhayfa رضي الله عنه said, "At the time of the Messenger of God ﷺ, a man would utter a word that would turn him into a hypocrite until he died. Nowadays, I hear such words from one of you ten times a day."[46]

One scholar said, "The nearest of people to hypocrisy are those who believe they are innocent of it."[47]

---

41 Al-Bukhārī, 34; and Muslim, 58.

42 A pure heart (*qalb ajrad*) means it is isolated from darkness. The bright light means it shines. See Abū Ṭālib al-Makkī, *Qūt al-qulūb*, 2:135.

43 Aḥmad b. Ḥanbal, *Musnad*, 3:17.

44 Aḥmad b. Ḥanbal, *Musnad*, 2:175. "By 'learned,' what is meant are the jurists: they will apply their knowledge in the wrong ways, and learn knowledge for the sake of their reputations, when in fact they do not believe in it. The hypocrites at the time of the Prophet ﷺ were the same way." Al-Zabīdī, *Itḥāf*, 2:270.

45 Abū Nuʿaym, *Ḥilya*, 7:112; and al-Ḍiyāʾ, *al-Aḥādīth al-mukhtāra*, 62.

46 Aḥmad b. Ḥanbal, *Musnad*, 5:390.

47 Abū Ṭālib al-Makkī, *Qūt al-qulūb*, 2:136.

Ḥudhayfa said, "There are more hypocrites today than there were at the time of the Messenger of God ﷺ. In those days they kept it hidden, while today they display it."[48]

This hypocrisy opposes the veracity and perfection of faith; yet it is hidden, and the furthest people from it are those who fear they might be guilty of it, while the nearest to it are those who believe they are innocent of it. Someone once said to Ḥasan al-Baṣrī, "People say that there is no more hypocrisy nowadays." He replied, "O brother, if the hypocrites were truly extinct, the streets would be empty."[49] It may have been he or someone else who said, "If hypocrites grew tails, we would no longer be able to sit down."[50]

Ibn ʿUmar رَضِيَ ٱللَّهُ عَنْهُمَا once heard a man speaking ill of al-Ḥajjāj. He said to him, "If he were here in person, would you speak ill of him?" The man said no. He said, "At the time of the Messenger of God ﷺ, we would call this hypocrisy.[51] The Prophet ﷺ said, 'If a man is two-tongued in this world, God will make him two-tongued in the hereafter.'"[52]

The Prophet ﷺ also said, "The most evil of people is the two-faced one, who shows one face to some people and the other to others."[53]

Someone said to Ḥasan رَحِمَهُ ٱللَّهُ, "Some people say that we need no longer fear hypocrisy." He replied, "By God, I would rather know that I am innocent of hypocrisy than possess enough gold to fill every mountain and valley in the world." Ḥasan also said, "Among the different forms of hypocrisy are disagreements between the tongue and the heart, the secret and the public, and the entrance and the exit." A man said to Ḥudhayfa رَضِيَ ٱللَّهُ عَنْهُ, "I fear that I am a hypocrite." He replied, "If you were a hypocrite, you would not fear that you are a hypocrite. The hypocrite is the one who feels safe from hypocrisy." Ibn Abī Mulayka said, "I met one hundred and

48 Al-Nasāʾī, 11531, and in a similar form by al-Bukhārī, 7113.

49 Abū Ṭālib al-Makkī, *Qūt al-qulūb,* 2:137. Al-Kharāʾiṭī reported a similar statement in *Musāwiʾ al-akhlāq*, 317.

50 Abū Ṭālib al-Makkī, *Qūt al-qulūb,* 2:137.

51 Ibn ʿAbd al-Barr, *al-Tamhīd*, 23:24; also, originally, al-Bukhārī, 7178.

52 Abū Nuʿaym, *Ḥilya*, 2:160.

53 Al-Bukhārī, 7179; and Muslim, 4715.

thirty Companions of the Prophet ﷺ, all of whom feared hypocrisy." One narration has "five hundred."[54]

It is related that the Messenger of God ﷺ was once sitting with a group of his Companions رضي الله عنهم when they mentioned a man and praised him greatly. As they were there, the man came along, his face dripping with water from his recent ablution. He was holding his sandals in his hand, and there was an imprint between his eyes from his frequent prostration. They said, "O Messenger of God, here is the man of whom we were speaking." He ﷺ said, "I see a mark of Satan on his face." The man approached, gave a greeting, and sat with the people. The Prophet ﷺ said to him, "I ask you in the name of God: when you approached the people, did the thought come to you that there was no one man among them better than you?" The man replied, "By my Lord, it did."[55]

The Prophet ﷺ once said in a supplication, "O God, I ask Your forgiveness for what I know, and what I know not." Someone said, "Do you fear, O Messenger of God?" He replied, "Why should I not, when the hearts are between two fingers of the All-Compassionate, who turns them whichever way He wills?"[56]

God سبحانه says, *and there will appear to them from God that which they had not taken into account* [39:47]. One interpretation of this is that some of the deeds which they did and deemed to be good will actually be counted against them as evil deeds.[57]

Sarī l-Saqaṭī said, "If a man were to enter a garden filled with all kinds of trees, upon each tree all manner of birds, and every bird were to address him in an intelligible language, saying, 'Peace be upon you, O Friend of God!', and his soul were to take pleasure in this, he would become a captive in their hands."[58]

---

54 See also Abū Ṭālib al-Makkī, *Qūt al-qulūb,* 2:137.

55 Abū Yaʿlā, *Musnad,* 90; Abū Nuʿaym, *Ḥilya,* 3:52; and al-Dāraquṭnī, 2:54.

56 The end of the narration is reported by Aḥmad b. Ḥanbal, *Musnad,* 2:250, and the beginning of it in Muslim, 4891, with the words, "O God, I seek refuge with You from the evil of what I have done and from the evil of what I have not done." The wording here is from Abū Ṭālib al-Makkī, *Qūt al-qulūb,* 2:138.

57 This is the interpretation of Mujāhid. Al-Qushayrī said concerning this verse, "Upon hearing this verse, people of vigilance become full of grief." See *Laṭāʾif al-ishārāt,* 3:285.

58 Abū Nuʿaym, *Ḥilya,* 10:118.

All these reports and traditions show you how dangerous this matter is because of the subtleties of hypocrisy and hidden idolatry, and that one can never be entirely safe from them. Even ʿUmar b. al-Khaṭṭāb رضي الله عنه used to ask Ḥudhayfa about himself and whether he was listed among the hypocrites.[59]

Abū Sulaymān al-Dārānī said, "I heard a certain ruler say something, and I wanted to criticize him, but I feared that he would order my execution. I did not fear death, but I feared that my heart would be embellished before the people in my moment of death. So I remained silent."[60]

This is the hypocrisy that opposes the reality of faith and its veracity, perfection, and purity, but not its basic presence.[61] Thus there are two kinds of hypocrisy: one that takes one out of the *dīn* and makes one a disbeliever on the path to an eternity in hell; and another that might cause one to enter hell for a time or to fall short of the highest stations of paradise and the rank of the veracious. This is a matter of doubt, which is why it is good to make a qualification [when declaring one's faith]. The root of this hypocrisy is the disparity between one's secret inner state and outward appearance, [or] feeling safe from God's planning, [being] self-satisfied, and other things of which only the veracious are innocent.

THE FOURTH JUSTIFICATION, again pertaining to doubt, is that [one makes this qualification] out of fear of what one's end might be, for one does not know if faith will last until the moment of death. If one's final end is disbelief, then any faith one might have had in the past is irrelevant, because faith only matters if it lasts until the end of life. If a man is fasting and is asked early in the day if he is fasting and says, "Yes, I am fasting," with complete confidence, and then breaks his fast before the day is out, his prior statement would become untrue because fasting is only valid when it is completed until sunset. Just as the daylight hours are the time wherein fasting is

59 Wakīʿ, *al-Zuhd*, 477; and Ibn ʿAsākir, *Tārīkh Dimashq*, 12:276.

60 Abū Ṭālib al-Makkī, *Qūt al-qulūb*, 2:137.

61 What is meant here is the hypocrisy of action that clouds the light of faith and makes it imperfect; although it is not as bad as hypocrisy in the creed, it is still a grave danger because it is a bridge that leads to it—may God give us refuge from that! This is true because becoming engrossed with God's favors can be a veil; Bishr b. al-Ḥārith said, "The heart's contentment with being praised is worse for it than sin."

completed, a person's lifetime is the time wherein faith is completed. If it is called valid before this time has run out, then this is only true based on the assumption that it will continue, which is a matter of doubt. The worst can always be feared for the final moment of life. It is for this reason that the God-fearing mostly weep, because it is the predestined fruit and the eternal will [of God], which can only be known at the moment when it comes to pass, and no man can predict it. Therefore fearing one's end is like fearing something that has already been ordained, and what is currently true may well be contradicted by what comes to pass in the future. Does anyone know if he is one of those for whom God has predestined goodness? It is said that God's تَعَالَىٰ words, *the intoxication of death will bring the truth* [50:19] mean "revealing what was predestined." One of the predecessors said, "Actions are only judged by their ends."[62]

Abū l-Dardāʾ رَضِيَ ٱللَّٰهُ عَنْهُ used to swear by God, saying, "If anyone feels secure that his faith will not be taken away, it will be taken away." It has been said that there are some sins that are punished with a difficult death—we seek God's refuge from that! It has been said that this is the punishment for laying a false claim to sainthood and miracles. One of the gnostics said, "If I were given the choice between dying as a martyr at the door of the house and dying as an ordinary believer in [God's] unity at the door of an inner room, I would choose the latter because I do not know if something might change my heart on the way to the door of the house." Another of them said, "If I knew a man to be a believer in [God's] unity for fifty years and then he were hidden from my sight by a pillar, and died, I would not be able to say with certainty that he died a believer in [God's] unity."[63]

A *ḥadīth* says, "Whoever says 'I am a believer' is a disbeliever; whoever says 'I am learned' is ignorant."[64]

It is said, about God's تَعَالَىٰ words, *and the word of your Lord has been fulfilled in truth and in justice* [6:115], that *in truth* refers

62 Narrated by Wahb b. Munabbih, see al-Suyūṭī, *al-Durr al-manthūr*, 3:418.

63 Abū Ṭālib al-Makkī, *Qūt al-qulūb*, 2:137.

64 Abū Ṭālib al-Makkī, *Qūt al-qulūb*, 2:138. The second statement in the narration is reported by al-Ṭabarānī, *al-Muʿjam al-awsaṭ*, 6842. In al-Ṭabarānī, *al-Muʿjam al-ṣaghīr*, 1:65, he states, "Whoever says, 'I am in the garden,' is in the fire." It is reported from Yaḥyā b. Abī Kathīr.

to those who die with faith while *in justice* refers to those who die in idolatry.[65] God also says, *and to God belongs the outcome of* [*all*] *matters* [22:41].

When the doubt is of this nature, it becomes obligatory to make the qualification, because faith means that which leads one to paradise. Fasting means being free of any blame concerning it, and if it is broken before sunset one is not free of blame. Thus it is no longer counted as a fast; and the same is true of faith. Indeed, even if someone were asked about a fast he performed yesterday, having no doubt that he completed it, it would not be out of place for him to answer, "Yes I did fast, God willing," because a true fast is the one that is accepted, and one can never be certain that one's deeds are accepted.

This shows that it is a good practice to qualify all of one's righteous deeds [by saying "God willing"] by way of expressing uncertainty as to whether they have been accepted or not. Even if they are performed correctly with all their outward conditions of validity met, there could be subtle reasons for them not to be accepted, known only to the glorious Lord of Lords. Thus it is good to be uncertain about them.

These are the justifications for qualifying one's answer to questions about one's faith; and with this, the *Book of the Principles of the Creed* is completed. God knows best.

This completes *Kitāb qawāʿid al-ʿaqāʾid,* which is the second book of the Quarter of Worship from the book, *The Revival of the Religious Sciences* (*Iḥyāʾ ʿulūm al-dīn*). All praise is for God, the Lord of the worlds. Blessings be on our master, Muḥammad, and on his pure family. It is followed by *Kitāb asrār al-ṭahāra* (*The Mysteries of Purification*)
Book 3

65 Abū Ṭālib al-Makkī, *Qūt al-qulūb*, 2:138.

Bibliography

Works in Western Languages

Blankinship, Khalid. "The Early Creed." In Tim Winter (ed.), *The Cambridge Companion to Classical Islamic Theology*, 33–54. Cambridge: Cambridge University Press, 2008.

Gimaret, D. "Muʿtazila." In *Encyclopaedia of Islam*, second edition, 7:783–793. Leiden: E. J. Brill, 1993.

Ibn al-Jawzī, ʿAbd al-Raḥmān b. ʿAlī. *Virtues of the Imām Aḥmad ibn Ḥanbal*. Edited and translated by Michael Cooperson, vol. 2. New York: New York University Press, 2015.

Ibn al-Nadīm, Muḥammad b. Isḥāq. *The Fihrist of al-Nadīm: A Tenth-Century Survey of Muslim Culture*. Translated by Bayard Dodge. New York: Columbia University Press, 1970.

Nasr, Seyyed Hossein and Oliver Leaman (eds.). *History of Islamic Philosophy*. New York: Routledge, 1996.

Patton, Walter M. *Aḥmed Ibn Ḥanbal and the Miḥna: A Biography of the Imâm Including an Account of the Moḥammedan Inquisition Called the Miḥna, 218–234, A.H.* Leiden: E. J. Brill, 1897.

Pavlin, James. "Sunni Kalam and Theological Controversies." In S. H. Nasr and O. Leaman (eds.), *History of Islamic Philosophy*, 1:105–118. London: Routledge, 1996.

Sharif, M. M. (ed.). *A History of Muslim Philosophy*. Wiesbaden: Otto Harrassowitz, 1963.

Watt, W. Montgomery. *Islamic Philosophy and Theology*. Edinburgh: Edinburgh University Press, 1985.

Works in Arabic

ʿAbd al-Razzāq b. Hammām al-Ṣanʿānī. *al-Muṣannaf*. Edited by Ḥabīb al-Raḥmān al-ʿAẓamī. Beirut: Maktab al-Islāmī, 1983.

Abū l-ʿAtāhiya, Ismāʿīl b. al-Qāsim b. Sūwayd. *Abū l-ʿAtāhiya ashʿārʾahu wa-akhbārahu*. Edited by Shukhrī Fayṣal. Damascus: Dār al-Mallāḥ, 1964.

Abū Dāwūd, Sulaymān b. al-Ashaʿth al-Sijistānī. *Sunan Abū Dāwūd*. Edited by ʿIzzat ʿAbīd al-Daʿās and ʿĀdil al-Sayyid. Beirut: Dār Ibn Ḥazm, 1997.

———. *al-Zuhd*. Edited by Yāsir b. Ibrāhīm and Ghanīm b. ʿAbbās. Cairo: Muʾassasat Abī ʿUbayda, 2010.

Abū Nuʿaym al-Iṣbahānī, Aḥmad b. ʿAbdallāh. *Ḥilyat al-awliyāʾ*. Cairo: Maṭbaʿāt al-Saʿāda wa-l-Khānijī, 1357/1938.

Abū Ṭālib al-Makkī, Muḥammad b. ʿAlī. *Qūt al-qulūb*. Cairo: al-Maṭbaʿat al-Maymaniyya, 1310/1892.

Abū Yaʿlā, Aḥmad b. ʿAlī. *Musnad Abū Yaʿlā l-Mawṣūlī*. Edited by Ḥusayn Salīm Asad al-Dārānī. Damascus: Dār al-Maʾmūn li-l-Turāth and Dār al-Thaqafa al-ʿArabiyya, 1989.

Aḥmad b. Ḥanbal. *Musnad al-Imām Aḥmad b. Ḥanbal*. Edited by Shuʿayb al-Arnāʾūṭ. Beirut: Muʾassasat al-Risāla, 1995.

al-Bayhaqī, Aḥmad b. al-Ḥusayn. *al-Madkhal ilā l-sunan al-kubrā = Sunan*. Edited by Muḥammad Ḍiyāʾ al-Raḥmān al-ʿĀẓamī. Medina: Dār Aḍwāʾ al-Salaf, 1420/1999.

———. *Shuʿab al-īmān*. Edited by Muḥammad al-Saʿīd b. Basyūnī Zaghlūl. Beirut: Dār al-Kutub al-ʿIlmiyyya, 2000.

al-Bukhārī, Muḥammad b. Ismāʿīl. *Ṣaḥīḥ al-Bukhārī*. Istanbul: n.p. [reprint of Beirut: Dār Ṭūq al-Najāt, 1422/2001].

al-Dāraquṭnī, ʿAlī b. ʿUmar. *Sunan al-Dāraquṭnī*. Edited by ʿAbdallāh Hashim Yamānī. Lebanon: Dār al-Maʿrifa, 1966 [repr.].

al-Dārimī, ʿAbdallāh b. ʿAbd al-Raḥmān. *Musnad al-Dārimī* [*Sunan*]. Edited by Ḥusayn Salīm Asad al-Dārānī. Riyadh: Dār al-Mughnī, 2000.

al-Daylamī, Shīrawayh b. Shahdār. *al-Firdaws bi-maʾthūr al-khiṭṭāb = Musnad al-firdaws*. Edited by Saʿīd b. Basyūnī Zaghlūl. Beirut: Dār al-Kutub al-ʿIlmiyya, 1986.

al-Dhahabī, Muḥammad b. Aḥmad. *Siyar aʿlām al-nubalāʾ*. Edited by Shuʿayb al-Arnāʾūṭ, et al. Beirut: Muʾassasat al-Risāla, 1996.

al-Ḍiyāʾ al-Dīn al-Maqdisī, Muḥammad b. ʿAbd al-Wāḥid. *al-Aḥādīth al-mukhtāra*. Edited by ʿAbd al-Malik ʿAbdallāh b. Dahīsh. Beirut: Dār Khiḍr, 2001.

al-Ghazālī, Abū Ḥāmid Muḥammad b. Muḥammad. *Faḍāʾiḥ al-Bāṭiniyya* ed Muḥammad ʿAlī l-Quṭb (Beirut and Sidon: al-Maktaba al-ʿAṣriyya, 2001).

———. *al-Imlāʾ ʿalā mushkil al-Iḥyāʾ*. Jedda: Dār al-Minhāj, 2011.

———. *al-Iqtiṣād fī l-iʿtiqād*. Edited by Anas Muḥammad ʿAdnān al-Sharfāwī. Jedda: Dār al-Minhāj, 2008.

———. *Maqṣad al-asnā*. Edited by Maḥmūd Bījū. Damascus: Maṭbʿat al-Ṣabāḥ, 1999.

———. *Mishkāt al-anwār*. Edited by ʿAbd al-ʿAzīz al-Sayrawān. Damascus: Dār al-Īmān, 1990.

———. *Mīzān al-ʿamal*. Edited by Sulaymān Dunyā. Cairo: Dār al-Maʿārif, 1964.

——. *al-Munqidh min al-ḍalāl*. Edited by Maḥmūd Bījū. Damascus: Maṭbʿat al-Ṣabāḥ, 1992.

——. *Qānūn al-taʾwīl*. Edited by Maḥmūd Bījū. Damascus: Maṭbʿat al-Ṣabāḥ, 1993.

——. *Tahāfut al-falāsifa*. Edited by Sulaymān Dunyā. Cairo: Dār al-Maʿārif, 1987.

Translations:

The Book of Knowledge. Translated by Kenneth Honerkamp. Louisville, KY: Fons Vitae, 2015.

al-Ghazālī's Moderation in Belief [a translation of *al-Iqtiṣād fī l-iʿtiqād*]. Translated by Aladdin M. Yaqub. Chicago: University of Chicago Press, 2013.

The Incoherence of the Philosophers: A Parallel English-Arabic Text. Translated by Michael E. Marmura. Provo, UT: Brigham Young University Press, 2000.

Letter to a Disciple. Translated by Tobias Mayer. Cambridge: Islamic Texts Society, 2005.

The Ninety-Nine Beautiful Names of God. Translated by David B. Burrell and Nazih Daher. Cambridge: Islamic Texts Society, 1992.

al-Ḥākim al-Nīsābūrī, Muḥammad b. ʿAbdallāh. *al-Mustadrak ʿalā l-Ṣaḥīḥayn*. Hyderabad: Dāʾirat al-Maʿārif al-Niẓāmiyya, 1335/1917 [repr. Beirut: Dār al-Maʿrifa, n.d.].

al-Ḥakīm al-Tirmidhī, Muḥammad b. ʿAlī. *Nawādir al-uṣūl*. Beirut: Dār Ṣādir, n.d. [reprint Cairo, 1293/1876 edition].

——. *Khatam al-awliyāʾ*. Edited by ʿUthmān Ismāʿīl Yaḥyā. Beirut: al-Maṭbaʿ al-Kāthūlīkīyya, 1965.

Ibn ʿAbbād, Ismāʿīl. *Dīwān Ṣāḥib b. ʿAbbād*. Edited by Muḥammad Ḥasan Āl Yāsīn. Beirut: Dār al-Qalam, n.d.

Ibn ʿAbd al-Barr, Yūsuf b. ʿAbdallāh. *Jāmiʿ bayān al-ʿilm wa-faḍlih*. Edited by Abū al-Ashbāl al-Zuhayrī. Riyadh: Dār Ibn al-Jawzī, 1994.

——. *al-Tamhīd*. Casablanca: Wizārat al-Awqāf, 1967.

Ibn Abī l-Sharīf, al-Kamāl. *Kitāb al-Musāmara fī sharḥ al-musāyira*. Cairo: Maṭbaʿat al-Saʿāda, 1347/1928.

Ibn Abī Shayba, ʿAbdallāh b. Muḥammad. *al-Muṣannaf*. Edited by Muḥammad ʿAwāmma. Jedda: Dār al-Minhāj, 2006.

Ibn ʿAsākir, ʿAlī b. al-Ḥasan. *Tārīkh Dimashq*. Edited by Muḥibb al-Dīn ʿUmar b. Gharāma al-ʿUmrāwī. Beirut: Dār al-Fikr, 1995.

Ibn al-Ḍarīs, Muḥammad b. Ayyūb. *Faḍāʾil al-Qurʾān*. Edited by Misfir b. Saʿīd al-Ghāmidī. Riyadh: Dār Ḥafiẓ, 1988.

Ibn Ḥibbān = Muḥammad b. Ḥibbān al-Bustī. *Ṣaḥīḥ Ibn Ḥibbān = al-Musnad al-ṣaḥīḥ ʿalā al-taqāsīm wa-l-ānwāʿ*. Edited by Aḥmad Shākir. Cairo: Dār al-Maʿārif, 1952.

Ibn Khallikān, Aḥmad b. Muḥammad. *Wafayāt al-aʿyān*. Edited by Iḥsān ʿAbbās. Beirut: Dār Ṣādir, 1968.

Ibn Māja, Muḥammad b. Yazīd. *Sunan Ibn Māja*. Edited by Muḥammad Fuʾād ʿAbd al-Bāqī. Cairo: Dār Iḥyāʾ al-Kutub al-ʿArabiyya, 1954.

al-Juwaynī, ʿAbdallāh b. Yūsuf. *al-Irshād ilā quwāṭaʿ al-adilla fī uṣūl al-ʿitiqād*. Edited by Muḥammad Yūsuf Mūsā and ʿAlī ʿAbd al-Munʿim ʿAbd al-Ḥamīd. Cairo: Maktabat al-Khanjī, 2002.

al-Kharāʾiṭī, Muḥammad b. Jaʿfar. *Musāwiʾ al-akhlāq*. Edited by Muṣṭafā ʿAṭā. Beirut: Muʾassasat al-Kutub al-Thaqāfiyya, 1993.

al-Khaṭīb al-Baghdādī, Aḥmad b. ʿAlī. *al-Faqīh wa-l-mutafaqqih*. Edited by ʿĀdil Yūsuf al-ʿAzāzī. Riyadh: Dār Ibn al-Jawzī, 1421/2000.

———. *Tārīkh Baghdād*. Edited by Muṣṭafā ʿAbd al-Qādir ʿAṭā. Beirut: Dār al-Kutub al-ʿIlmiyya, 1997.

al-Lālakāʾī, Hibat Allāh b. al-Ḥasan. *Sharḥ uṣūl iʿtiqād ahl al-sunna*. Edited by Aḥmad Saʿd al-Ghāmidī. Riyadh: Dār Ṭayyiba, 2005.

al-Mundharī, ʿAbd al-ʿAẓīm b. ʿAbd al-Qawī. *al-Targhīb wa-l-tarhīb*. Edited by Muḥyī l-Dīn Mistū, Samīr al-ʿAṭṭār, and Yūsuf Badawī. Damascus: Dār Ibn Kathīr, 1999.

Muslim b. al-Ḥajjāj al-Qushayrī l-Nīsābūrī. *Ṣaḥīḥ Muslim*. Edited by Muḥammad Fuʾād ʿAbd al-Bāqī. Cairo: Dār Iḥyāʾ al-Kutub al-ʿArabiyya, 1954.

al-Nasāʾī, Abū ʿAbd al-Raḥmān Aḥmad b. Shuʿayb. *Sunan al-Nasāʾī*. Cairo: al-Maṭbaʿat al-Maymaniyya, 1312/1894.

al-Qushayrī, ʿAbd al-Karīm. *Laṭāʾif al-ishārāt*. Edited by Ibrāhīm al-Basyūnī. Cairo: al-Hayāʾ al-Miṣriyya al-ʿĀmma, 1981.

———. *al-Risāla al-Qushayriyya*. Edited by ʿAbd al-Ḥalīm Maḥmūd and Maḥmūd b. al-Sharīf. Cairo: Dār al-Shaʿab, 1989.

al-Subkī, ʿAbd al-Wahhāb b. ʿAlī. *Ṭabaqāt al-shāfiʿīya al-kubrā*. Edited by Maḥmūd Muḥammad al-Ṭanāḥī and ʿAbd al-Fattāḥ al-Ḥilū. Cairo: Dār Iḥyāʾ al-Kutub al-ʿArabiyya, 1396/1976.

al-Sulamī, Abū ʿAbd al-Raḥmān. *al-Arbaʿīn fī l-taṣawwuf*. Hyderabad: Majlis Dāʾirat al-Maʿārif al-ʿUthmānīya, 1981.

al-Suyūṭī, ʿAbd al-Raḥmān b. Abī Bakr. *al-Durr al-manthūr fī l-tafsīr bi-maʾthur*. Beirut: Dār al-Fikr, 2002.

al-Ṭabarānī, Sulaymān b. Aḥmad. *al-Muʿjam al-awsaṭ*. Edited by Maḥmūd al-Ṭaḥḥān. Riyadh [?]: Maktabat al-Maʿārif, 1985.

———. *al-Muʿjam al-kabīr*. Edited by Ḥamdī ʿAbd al-Majīd al-Salafī. Beirut: Dār Iḥyāʾ al-Turāth al-ʿArabī, n.d.

———. *al-Muʿjam al-ṣaghīr*. Beirut: Dār al-Kutub al-ʿIlmiyya, 1983 [repr.].

al-Ṭabarī, Muḥammad b. Jarīr. *Tafsīr al-Ṭabarī = Jāmiʿ al-bayān*. Beirut and Amman: Dār Ibn Ḥazm and Dār al-ʿĀlam, 2002.

al-Thaʿālibī, ʿAbd al-Malik b. Muḥammad Abū Manṣūr. *Yatīmat al-dahr*. Edited by Mufīd Muḥammad Qamīḥa. Beirut: Dār al-Kutub al-ʿIlmiyya, 1983.

al-Tirmidhī, Muḥammad b. ʿĪsā. *Sunan al-Tirmidhī = al-Jāmiʿ al-ṣaḥīḥ*. Edited by Aḥmad Shākir, Muḥammad Fuʾād ʿAbd al-Bāqī, and Ibrāhīm ʿAṭwa. Beirut: Dār Iḥyāʾ al-Turāth al-ʿArabī, n.d. [reprint of Cairo, 1938 edition].

al-ʿUqaylī, Muḥammad b. ʿAmr. *al-Ḍuʿafāʾ*. Edited by Ḥamdī ʿAbd al-Majīd al-Salafī. Riyadh: Dār al-Ṣamīʿī, 2000.

Wakīʿ b. al-Jarrāḥ al-Rūʾāsī. *al-Zuhd*. Edited by ʿAbd al-Raḥmān ʿAbd al-Jabbār al-Fariwāʾī. Riyadh: Dār al-Ṣumaʿī, 1994.

al-Yāfiʿī, ʿAbdallāh b. Asʿad. *Mirʾāt al-jinān wa-ʿibrat al-yaqẓān*. Hyderabad: Maṭbaʿat Dāʾirat al-Maʿarif al-Niẓāmiyya, 1918–1920.

al-Zabīdī, Muḥammad Murtaḍā, *Itḥāf al-sadā l-muttaqīn bi-sharḥ Iḥyāʾ ʿulūm al-dīn*. [Cairo]: al-Maṭbaʿ al-Maymūniyya, 1311/1894.

Index of Qur᾿ānic Verses

Index of *Ḥadīth*

General Index

ʿAbbāsid (caliphate), xiv, xxiii
ablutions, 113. *See also* prayers
Abraham, 31, 70
abstract (concepts), 51
Abū Bakr al-Ṣiddīq, 20, 27, 43, 47, 87
Abū Bakr b. al-ʿArabī, xvii
Abū l-Dardāʾ, 115
Abū Hāshim, 38
Abū Hurayra, 43, 49
Abū Jahl, 79
Abū Saʿīd al-Khudrī, 111
Abū Sulaymān al-Dārānī, 114
Abū Yūsuf, 30
accidents, xxviii, 4, 6, 12, 14, 58, 64, 65
acquisition, xxv, 76
acts/actions, xx, xxvi, 2, 46, 57, 69–70, 75, 78, 96, 102–105, 110–111, 115. *See also* deeds
  and faith, 96, 101
  human, xxviii, 58
  of God, xxvii–xxviii, 14, 58, 75, 84
  of obedience, 80, 102, 104, 110
  of worship, 25–26, 96, 98
  righteous, 95, 105, 116
  voluntary (*sunan*), 103
admonitions/counsel, 37
adultery, 47, 96, 105
adults/adulthood, 80–81
affirmation, 61–62, 99
ʿĀʾisha, 32, 33
ʿAlī b. Abī Ṭālib, xxiii–xxiv, 20, 32–33, 41–42, 87–88, 105
allegiance, 87, 89
ʿAlqama, 107
analogies, 14, 31, 82, 99
angels, xxii, 10, 14, 33, 93, 97, 107
animals, 14, 60, 70, 75, 79
  ants, 65, 70, 111
  bats, 47
  bees, 75
  birds, 86, 113
  donkeys, 49
  dung beetles, 47
  lions, 82–83, 86
  pigs/swine, 48
  ram, 80, 108
  spiders, 75
annihilation, 85
apostasy/apostates, xxv, 57, 101
aptitude, 27, 41
Arabs, 16, 84
arguments/argumentation, 26, 31, 34–37, 71, 111. *See also* debate
arrogance, 31
ascendancy, of God, 54, 66–67
ascension, of the Prophet, 55
asceticism, 29
al-Ashʿarī, Abū l-Ḥasan, 55, 101

competence, 89
compliance, 92
compulsion, 76, 78
conduct, 109. *See also* acts; deeds
  correct/proper, xx, 103
confirmation (ʿ*aqd*), 95
conjunction, vs. separation, 64
consensus, 87, 96
consideration, and realization, 82
contingency(ies), 61, 66, 72
  independence from, 62–63, 72
contingent, 31, 60–62, 64–65
  beings/entities, 14, 60–61, 63–64, 72–73, 75
  power, 71
  states, 61, 63
control, 8, 70, 77, 79
conviction(s), xxvii, xxix, 25, 35, 37, 97, 103–104
corruption, 29, 36, 38, 110
countenance, of God, 6, 47
covenants, 110–111
craftsman/producer, 70
creation, xxvi, 6, 60, 64, 68–69, 85
  of God, 75–76
  of the universe, 79
  organization of, 69
creatures, 59
  of God, 8, 12, 16, 71, 73, 75, 82
creed(s), xxi, xxvi, xxviii, 2, 25–26, 36–38, 41, 45, 56, 57, 80, 103
  hypocrisy in, 114
  moderation in, 76
  principles of, xxiii–xxiv, 38, 89

Damascus, xv, xvii
dark/darkness, 2, 8, 12, 18, 51, 70, 111
day, xxi, 59, 114
death, xviii, 18, 34, 51, 59, 62, 83, 96, 114–115
debate, xxvii, 25–27, 29, 31–33, 35, 37. *See also* arguments
deception/lies, 40, 111
decrees, 14
deeds, 18, 20, 28, 75–76, 93–94, 99–102, 113. *See also* acts; conduct
  acceptence of, 116
  of humankind/servants, 76–77
  records of, 86
deficiencies, 70, 75, 103
delusion, 70
descent (of God), 54
design (of God), 75
desire(s), 40, 51, 82–83, 109
devils/Devil, 10, 14, 77
devotions, 26, 28
direction(s), xxviii, 64–68
disbelief/disbelievers, xxvi, 20, 31–32, 43–45, 47–48, 50, 81–82, 95, 98, 100–101, 106, 108–109, 114–115
disobedience, 77, 97, 100
dissimulation, 103
divinity, 64
dominion, 75
doubt(s), xxix, 2, 33, 35, 37–41, 88, 99, 101, 103–104, 106–109, 114, 116

earth(s), 4, 6, 14, 18, 43, 52, 59–60, 68, 72, 75, 86
education, xiii, xvi, xxvii
elite, xxvii, 45, 103
eloquence, 84
endlessness (of the Creator), 61
error, 70, 77
essence, 31, 52, 64
  of God, xxvi, xxviii, 2, 4, 6, 8, 10, 12, 14, 52, 57–58, 71–73
eternality, 61, 63
  of God, xxviii, 63
eternal (*qadam*/*qadīm*), 62–63, 71–73
  attributes (of God), 74
  existence (of God), 63
  God is, 4
  knowledge (of God), 8, 73
  originator, 62

About the Translator

Khalid Williams studied Arabic and Islamic studies at the University of Leeds; he graduated in 2005 and moved to Morocco to continue his study of traditional Islamic sciences and spirituality in Salé, Fes, Oujda, and Nador. His previous translations include *Our Master Muhammad: The Messenger of Allah* by Imam ʿAbdallah Sirajuddin al-Husayni; *Muḥammad the Perfect Man* by Sayyid Muḥammad ibn ʿAlawī al-Mālikī al-Ḥasanī; *Love in the Holy Qurʾan* by HRH Prince Ghazi bin Muhammad; *The Qurʾān and the Prophet in the Writings of Shaykh Aḥmad al-ʿAlawī*; and the *Dalāʾil al-Khayrāt* of Imām Jazūlī. He has also translated Book 9 of the *Revival of the Religious Sciences* (*Iḥyāʾ ʿulūm al-dīn*): *Invocations and Supplications*. He lives in Salé, Morocco with his family.

About the Reviewer

James Pavlin recieved his PhD from New York University. He is an adjunct professor in the history department at William Paterson University (New Jersey) and a part time lecturer in the department of religion at Rutgers University. He is the author of *Ibn Taymiya's Epistle on Worship: Risālat al-ʿubūdiyya*. He has written extensively on the Muslim creed, *kalām*, and its relation to Islamic philosophy. For this work he reviewed the translation against the Arabic text, provided a translation of many of the footnotes, and wrote an early draft of the introduction. He has also translated Book 8 of the *Revival of the Religious Sciences* (*Iḥyāʾ ʿulūm al-dīn*): *The Etiquette of the Recitation of the Qurʾān*. He is currently working on a translation of Book 19: *The Commanding of Right and the Forbidding of Wrong*.

This publication was made possible through the generosity of international donors and through the support of a grant from the John Templeton Foundation. The opinions expressed in this publication are those of its authors and do not necessarily reflect the views of the John Templeton Foundation.